WITH GRATITUDE

to the One Mind
which revealed Its Presence and Truth
through the receptive consciousness of

Thomas Hora

a true physician of the soul,
one who heeded Christ's words:
"Physician, heal thyself" (Lk. 4:23).

Susan von Reichenbach is a longtime student of Metapsychiatry,
having mentored many years with Dr. Hora in New York City.
She is the editor of Dr. Hora's book, "One Mind," and is
a spiritual guide in Metapsychiatry and a Meta-class teacher.

Susan is a graduate of Sarah Lawrence College, where Joseph Campbell, her tutor and advisor,
had a significant influence on her early path.
She has enjoyed an international career as an opera and concert singer.

Susan can be reached by mail at P.O. Box 1024, Old Lyme, CT 06371 USA,
by telephone at 860.405.4044 or by email at
metabooks@metapsychiatry.info

Meta Meanings has a companion book, **Meta Prayers and Principles**.
Information regarding book orders, and other articles,
can be found at the website:

www.TheMetaWay.com

Would you like to liberate yourself
from the lower realms of life?
Would you like to save the world
from the degradation and destruction
it seems to be destined for?
Then step away from the shallow mass
movements
and quietly go to work on your self-
awareness.

If you want to awaken all of humanity,
then awaken all of yourself.
If you want to eliminate the suffering in the
world,
then eliminate all that is dark
and negative in yourself.
Truly, the greatest gift you have to give
Is that of your own self-transformation.

— *Lao-tze*

To straighten the crooked
You must first do a harder thing –
Straighten yourself.

— *Buddha*

A man's foes will be those of his own
household.

— *Jesus Christ, Mt. 10:36*

You are here for your own salvation.

— *Thomas Hora, M.D.*

Table of Contents

Definitions of Words Often Used in Metapsychiatry

Definitions of Words Often Juxtaposed in Metapsychiatry

Prologue

This booklet was inspired by a desire to offer a helpful resource to the students of Meta who work with me and any other seekers who might find it so. It aims to clarify Metapsychiatry's most basic concepts, its unique terminology and some of its definitions, as well as to explicate its approach to problem solving through a method of juxtaposing ideas. The language of Metapsychiatry is vast. Therefore, the vocabulary chosen within this booklet can describe only the foundation stones ("basic stuff") of Metapsychiatry's literature. For instance, words like *self-confirmatory ideation* and *operationalism* can be stumbling blocks without sufficient definitions to help us grasp their full meaning. The insights and clarifications incorporated into this booklet were expressed by Dr. Hora and are scattered throughout the teaching like shining threads. The task was to gather up and "sew" these threads of light ("sutras")[1] into a small but handy tapestry; it is hoped that this "tapestry" may prove useful as a study tool or reference manual for teachers and students alike. It intends, at all times, to capture the precision of Dr. Hora's written and spoken words and to adhere to the purity and spirit of Metapsychiatry's semantics and ideation. This primer, then, a companion to Metapsychiatry's literature, aims not only to preserve as faithfully as possible some of the extraordinary wealth of ideas that streamed through Dr. Hora's capacious consciousness, but also to facilitate and accelerate understanding and integration of Metapsychiatry's body of knowledge. It is meant to act as a guide through the Metapsychiatric terrain, highlighting and clarifying its central ideas and the language which offer a pathway to enlightenment. Hopefully, this companion book will serve to make this glorious teaching more "effortless, effective and efficient"[2] to apprehend for all its adherents and, thus, to make the dialogic process more fruitful.

If you want to understand complexity,
You will need to see the simple things that it contains.
Then the great will be small,
The complex will be simple,
Effort will vanish,
And all things will arrange themselves in order.

— Lao-tze

---

[1] The word *sutras* translates from the Sanskrit to mean "threads," "phrases of words," ergo, the Vedic Sutras are so named because they are a collection of "sacred threads." The word suture, used in the medical profession, finds it origin in this word. Hence, healing threads can be invisible as well as visible.

[2] The "three Es."

We can never reconcile an All-Loving God with certain phenomena of the human condition — with violence, wars, terrorism, murder, economic collapse, disease, epidemics, poverty, pollution, so-called "natural" disasters, severe weather conditions or unexpected calamities. These phenomena are not random acts of God nor divine chastisements nor the work of an evil power. A supremely loving God knows nothing of these occurrences. There is no mystery to these events: they are the outpicturing of mankind's harmful collective thought-energies, the binding together of huge amounts of ignorant thoughts, which accumulate and then explode into the world as the phenomena we experience. These thoughts begin in our individual consciousness (in our "household"). Just as energies with similar properties tend to synergize, similar thoughts also tend to synergize with other like-minded thoughts, and then they take visible form as conflict and destruction in our world. So every time we entertain hurtful, angry, critical, judgmental, controlling, greedy, materialistic, jealous or malicious thoughts (from the "sea of mental garbage") or are estranged from God, we are individually contributing to the planet's demise.

And the leaves of the tree were for the healing of the nations. — Rev. 22:2

However, it is not the will of God that Its creation suffer — not ever. For God is a Principle of nondual Good, which means Its Goodness has no opposite — there is neither suffering nor any darkness in It. Therefore, it is necessary to correct our lack of understanding about events in the human condition. Harmful and destructive events and experiences do not find their source in God, but in our distorted thoughts. We need to acknowledge that in the Universe of Mind, which is divine Reality, there is no suffering (no fear, no disease, no war, no terrorist, no weapon of mass destruction, no "evil"). Then we need to clarify for ourselves that these are the phenomena of ignorance. Although impressive and disturbing, they are nonetheless just an appearance of highly-charged hostile thoughts, manifesting the mental "garbage" which constitutes the global consciousness. Metapsychiatry directs us to see rightly: we do not get involved in how we want the world to be or not to be; we do not get sick over the world condition, nor do we run away from it. Instead we establish the truth of God's perfect spiritual Universe in our own consciousness; and each time we are able to do this, each time we can see "what really is" — God's perfect creation — we are contributing to the healing of the world through our own transformation. We pray for the world in this way, first confronting the contents of our own consciousness, cleansing it and healing it, knowing that God is unconditional Love, and beholding the world as within God's perfect governance, regardless of appearances to the contrary. Contemplating the Prayer of Beholding[1] enables us to see beyond the picture. And the "leaves of the tree" give us a message about harmonious coexistence: there is neither friction of interaction among leaves, nor rivalry nor greed, nor do leaves have a desire for a relationship with other leaves nor for control over one another. The leaves let one another be, and they all find their source peacefully in the same tree. This metaphor points to the Principle of Omniaction wherein "the healing of the nations" can occur.

---

[1] "Everything everywhere is already all right."

Introduction

Metapsychiatry ("beyond" psychiatry) is a spiritual teaching founded by New York psychiatrist, Thomas Hora, a pioneer researcher into consciousness, whose work transcended traditional psychiatry. It is based on a metaphysical concept of human beings, seen wholly in the spiritual context of the Divine Creator. It draws liberally from the existential teachings of the Christ, the Buddha, Zen masters and the wisdom of mystics and philosophers of all ages, as well as from the discoveries of quantum physics, to illuminate its unique approach to the realization of our already-existing wholeness. This teaching is concerned with exploring ideas which substantiate the realm of consciousness as the only reality, the instrument of our enlightenment through which the healing of our bodies, experiences and relationships can occur, individually and collectively. The body is the vehicle of consciousness and, as such, is valuable in helping us to realize transcendence of our passage through the material experience. The purpose of our lives is to awaken to our eternal and inseparable divinity within the Divine Presence, to know it consciously and to manifest it consciously as fully as possible. In Dr. Hora's own words,

> Metapsychiatry came into the world to put soul into psychiatry,
> and to breathe the life of Spirit into the 'valley of dry bones.' (Ez. 37:1-6)

Central to Meta-teaching is the idea that thoughts manifest as our reality. Essentially, our every experience is an outpicturing of a conscious or unconscious thought — whether in individual experience or in the collective, global experience. "We live in a mental universe," said Dr. Hora, "and thought is the basic stuff of life."[1] Metapsychiatry defines a thought as *a unit of energy.* Based on the Second Law of Thermodynamics, which informs us that energy can be neither created nor destroyed, but it can be transmuted, we can see that our thoughts tend to take visible form (transmute) as our difficulties, problems, sicknesses, symptoms, pain and disease, as our financial, psychological, emotional, marital or family suffering, as our disappointments, disturbances and frustrations, even as our wars and so-called natural disasters, or — depending on the kind of thought-energies we are entertaining — as our overall well-being and harmonious prospering, individually and globally. Our consciousness directly affects the affairs of our lives in the visible world and shapes the events of the universe.

> As you sow [in thought], so shall you reap [in experience]. (Gal. 6:7)

We call this dynamic the Law of Correspondence. It is important to note Metapsychiatry's radical understanding that we are not producers of thoughts but receivers of them. Thoughts "obtain" (are received). Metapsychiatry identifies two sources of all the thoughts we can receive: the "sea of mental garbage" — the source of self-confirmatory ideation — and the "Ocean of Love-Intelligence" — the source of God-confirmatory ideation. Apprehending this revolutionary idea, that thoughts are received into consciousness rather than generated by it, is critical. It depersonalizes the darkness of ignorance, so there can be no personal blame or guilt attached to mistakes and wrongdoing — and it depersonalizes the brilliance of divine love and wisdom, so there can be no personal credit or self-glorification attached to the good, inspired and intelligent ideas which demonstrate

---

[1] Einstein's equation e=mc² affirms that energy and matter are the same substance, transmuted.

the activity of the divine Mind descending into human consciousness, blessing us. Given this understanding, Metapsychiatry places great importance on examining the thoughts we "obtain and entertain," and alerts us to their tendency to attract corresponding experiences into our lives. It encourages us to make conscious use of our troubles and illnesses so that we can uncover the hidden thoughts which they conceal. Once the thoughts are corrected and healed (using the two-step method of the Two Intelligent Questions)[1], our difficulties and infirmities can also be healed, once and for all. The "same old" patterns disappear; chronic ailments dissolve.

Metapsychiatry offers us a system of truth-realization which makes use of a very specific method of juxtaposition, also known as the "dialectic of juxtaposition" or "cognitive dialectics." This method does not use a process of elimination to discover truth, nor is it about opposites: instead, this method of juxtaposition places "garbage ideas" side by side with divine ideas, in order to illustrate the contrast between them. It is the contrast that exposes an illusion or lie, a false value or distorted viewpoint; in the instant when some aspect of truth — the real — is able to be seen, the lie is uncovered. When we are able to apprehend the real ("what really is"), the false disappears. For instance, if we were universally hypnotized to believe that 2 + 2 = 5, and we based all our computations on that belief, no matter how hard we tried, there could never be harmony or order or the right answer in our computations — and we would never know why. If, however, some wise mathematician were to come along and inform us that we had a mistaken notion — that actually 2 + 2 = 4 — and if we were interested in putting the new idea into practice, we would discover that it was the truth. The correct formula does indeed bring harmony and order and the right solution to our computations. In the moment that we would be able to recognize the truth of the new formula, seeing the evidence of its presence as it corrects the problem in our computations, we would naturally begin to use it to replace our habitual, but erroneous, premise.

Lies, therefore, can be useful," as Dr. Hora noted.

> Leaning on the worldly experience can be helpful
> in revealing the existence of some aspect of truth
> in juxtaposition to it. (Thomas Hora)

So it is that Metapsychiatry offers us an existential education to supersede our universal miseducation. It is "the wise mathematician" who corrects our most basic and false formulas, our illusory beliefs and misperceptions about who and what we are, our mistaken ideas about the nature and purpose of our existence, and our limited understanding of what God is. The new formula reveals the hidden truth of being, and opens the way for us to see it.

> For nothing is covered that will not be revealed,
> or hidden that will not be known. (Mt. 10:26)

The juxtapositional approach is ancient. It finds its origins in the biblical writings of John who expressed the idea that light cannot reveal itself without darkness, nor spirit without matter, and it was later reinforced by Meister Eckhart, 14th century mystic and priest, in his use of the "via negativa" to reveal the "via positiva." But Metapsychiatry's contribution of the Two Intelligent Questions[2] to facilitate this particular approach and

---

[1] See page 18 of this book for an explanation.
[2] See page 18 of this book for an explanation.

uncover *meanings* is unique — it is pivotal to the success of the teaching. The Two Intelligent Questions guide us to recognize the presence of harmful or pathogenic thoughts in our consciousness in a precise and meaningful way, and then lead us to replace and erase them with beneficial, spiritual thoughts which bless us. Every time the mental equivalent of a problem or symptom is revealed, the problem or symptom is being converted or transmuted from matter back into energy (using Einstein's equation), i.e., back to the specific thought being entertained. When that troublesome thought is replaced by a divine idea, the troublesome form (problem or symptom) can disappear. This is a powerful, alchemical process which Metapsychiatry offers: it is a process which occurs in consciousness, whereby Truth is moving miraculously across substances to transform them. We come to see that the tangible is insubstantial, and the intangible is the only real substance. At first this approach can seem revolutionary to our thinking and even appear abstract, but we can come to see that applying the juxtapositional method is highly practical. Learning to make use of it enables us to live with more ease and effectiveness in the world. We can be healed, and our experiences, one by one, can be transformed as they mirror back to us the specific thoughts that need to be corrected. In this way, our lives can be qualitatively improved, and we can come to know an harmonious and impeccable existence. Timeless wisdom supports this Meta-discipline.

Christ gave us a revelatory metaphor with these words,

> First cleanse the inside of the cup and of the plate,
> that the outside also may be clean. (Mt. 23:25)

This metaphor illustrates the correspondence between the thoughts we entertain inwardly in the "cup" of consciousness and that which we experience outwardly in our individual lives. In the same vein, Meister Eckhart elucidated,

> The soul reveals itself not by addition but through subtraction.

As we gradually "subtract" the mental clutter from our consciousness (our "cup"), our spiritual essence reveals itself to be already aligned with God — there is no longer anything interfering with its ability to shine forth. And in the Tao Te Ching, Lao-tze teaches us,

> When you discard the false, you will have room for the true…
> The Way to Life opens without effort.

It is thus that we can realize our divine being and our highest purpose: to let the One Life live through us and show forth what we already are.

Susan von Reichenbach
Spring 2006

Consciousness

Consciousness is a nondimensional entity of awareness, an individualized aspect of Cosmic Consciousness (a synonym for Reality) which has the faculty of being aware of being aware; consciousness is what we are as well as the true Realm in which we exist eternally; it is the nonmaterial, the indestructible, eternal essence and real substance of man which is spirit; it is synonymous with the "living soul" (Gn. 2:7); it is the "I am" of the Universal "I AM" (Ex. 3:14). In the language of quantum mechanics, it is "pure Being" — the Being of our being.

Every individual is an infinite consciousness within the Infinite Divine Consciousness, and all that is needed comes from this Consciousness. Consciousness is the aspect of the Divine which we have in common with It. It is our true identity. (The word identity, from Latin, *idem*, means the "same" or "like.") Thus, like its Source, consciousness is incorporeal, cannot be localized and has no shape: it is undefined, indefinite and infinite; it is birthless, deathless, and survives the body. The concept of consciousness replaces the illusion of a personal mind which believes it can produce thoughts and has a personal willpower. Consciousness does not think or produce ideas — thoughts and ideas *obtain* (are received) in consciousness (which is what gives us the false impression that we think). Just as a radio does not produce music, but receives it, the nature of consciousness is also designed to receive — it is designed to receive the wholly good, perfectly loving, supremely intelligent ideas from the "Ocean of Love-Intelligence," to receive Its wisdom, inspiration, creativity, joy, peace, protection and divine impulses, so that we can be guided and governed spiritually every moment of our lives. (Unfortunately, we can also receive ideas from the world's "sea of mental garbage," until we are sufficiently awake to be able to distinguish and separate the "garbage" thoughts from those ideas emanating from the "Ocean of Love-Intelligence" and refuse entry to the "garbage.") Consciousness, then, is the transparent receiver through which the One Mind or Divine Consciousness can reach us, fill us and flow through us into the world. Dr. Hora once said, "Without consciousness, man is nothing but decaying matter." Grasping this truth helps us to see beyond our physical appearances to our invisible divine identity as an entity of awareness. The ways in which consciousness expresses awareness are as follows: consciousness can be aware of itself being aware, aware of the thoughts it entertains, aware of what is going on around it in the world, aware of truth and ignorance, and, at its highest point of evolution, aware of God and able to behold Its divine Presence and activity everywhere and in every life form. The beholder in consciousness is called the *transcendent observer*, and it has the faculty of *spiritual discernment*: it can differentiate between that which is spiritual and true (existentially valid) and that which is illusory and false (existentially invalid). The *transcendent observer* sees from an ascendant, nonjudgmental perspective; it does not see persons or problems; it does not interact or react; it is neither active nor passive, and it is not fooled. The *transcendent observer* observes experiential life with benevolence and compassion, without being too interested or involved in it. This faculty of awareness is a clarifier: it sees issues and ideas and is responsive to manifest needs. The fully awakened *transcendent observer* is synonymous with the Christ-consciousness.

There is no separation between consciousness and its divine Source — there is only the One, and we are Its individuations. We are in It, and It is in us: we are each the Allness of God, manifesting individually. Today's science calls this the holographic model — the whole is contained in its every part; likewise, the entire Cosmic Consciousness — which is God, which is Love-Intelligence, which is Spiritual Reality — is contained in every individual consciousness. The ocean is in the wave; the tree is in the leaf; the entire oak tree is in the acorn; the Kingdom of God is within each of Its manifestations — that is each of us. The Infinite is in the finite in every moment. All that is needed to access It is to become aware of It, and it is because we are consciousness that we are able to do this. The ancient texts of the Upanishads describe the whole universe as One Reality and that Reality as pure consciousness. Metapsychiatry is interested in awakening receptive individuals from the dream of life as persons — as bodies, as clothes, as jobs, as money, as sex, as experiences — in order to see and to know their spiritual essence as consciousness, eventually to realize their own indwelling Christ-consciousness. "To them that received him [the Christ's enlightened understanding], gave the the power to be the children of God...   born not of blood....but of God" (Jn. 1:12-13).

It is worth noting that *consciousness* and the *contents of consciousness* are not the same and are not to be confused as synonymous. Consciousness is the vessel, the unseen "cup," which is a receiver of ideas. But, the contents of consciousness are the ideas we choose to entertain, in other words, the particular thoughts present in our cup (which can emanate from either the "sea of mental garbage" or the "Ocean of Love-Intelligence"). The quality of our consciousness, therefore, determines the quality of our lives and experiences, and influences the events of the universe. "As within, so without." Therefore, it is vitally important to understand that everything depends upon the nature of the thoughts we entertain (the contents of our consciousness). For the Buddha informs us: "You are what you think, having become what you thought." And the Bible instructs us, "That which has been [the thoughts we entertained in the past] is [what we are experiencing] now; that which is to be [what we will experience in the future], hath already been [is already present in the contents of our consciousness]; and God requireth that which is past" (Ecc. 3:15). To surrender the past, we must become *stewards of consciousness* and learn to cleanse the contents of our consciousness regularly. We will thus be able to release the old, existentially invalid content to God to be obliterated, as our thoughts are corrected, healed, and replaced by new and spiritually valid thoughts. Gaining *dominion* over the contents of our consciousness, we are able to be fully present in the eternal Now, and thereby accessible to God. Our consciousness is then freed to serve its highest purpose — being "here for God."

Divine Love-Intelligence

Divine Love-Intelligence is a wholly benevolent mental Force, which operates independent of man (i.e., man does not influence It); It is a cosmic Principle and an existential synonym for God, so-named to identify God's primary attributes.

The qualities of perfect Love and supreme Intelligence constitute the substance of Reality, and they cannot be separated. (Love is always supremely intelligent, and Intelligence is always perfectly loving.) Love and intelligence do not originate inside of us as personal traits — we do not produce them, and, therefore, we cannot take credit for them. We are spiritual beings, reflections of Love-Intelligence, and our love, our intelligence and our vitality have a transcendent derivative. The qualities of love and intelligence are spiritual, expressions of the Divine, flowing to us and shining through us, guiding and governing our lives, maintaining, sustaining, permeating and animating all life. It is essential to have a spiritually mature concept of what God is if we are finally to realize ourselves as Its "image" and "likeness" (Gn. 1:26). Since we are "defined by God" (and not the other way around), we must endeavor to have a real understanding of the nature of God, of what God really is, and how divine laws and principles operate — otherwise we can never know our authentic being. Therefore, we must move away from the tendency to anthropomorphize God (to see God as wearing a necktie or a skirt) or to conceive of this Presence as dimensional, material, finite or limited, or to ascribe to It any human characteristics. This Presence is not outside of us — It is in us, as Consciousness, and, as consciousness, we are in It. "I am in the Father [divine Love-Intelligence], and the Father [divine Love-Intelligence] is in me" (Jn. 14:11). It helps us to know God by other names as a way to expand our understanding beyond our limited human perception of what God is. In Metapsychiatry, we also refer to God as: Omniactive Love-Intelligence, One Mind, One Life, Being, Divine Mind, Universe of Mind, Infinite Creative Mind, I AM Presence, Eternal Now, Cosmic Consciousness, Reality, Divine Reality, Spiritual Reality, Infinite Reality, Truth, Fundamental Order of Existence, Is Principle, All-in-all (and quantum physics also contributes to this spiritualized vocabulary, calling God, "Nonlocal Mind"). understanding beyond our limited human perception of what God is. In Metapsychiatry, we also refer to God as: Omniactive Love-Intelligence, One Mind, One Life, Being, Divine Mind, Universe of Mind, Infinite Creative Mind, I AM Presence, Eternal Now, Cosmic Consciousness, Reality, Divine Reality, Spiritual Reality, Infinite Reality, Truth, Fundamental Order of Existence, Is Principle, All-in-all (and quantum physics also contributes to this spiritualized vocabulary, calling God, "Nonlocal Mind").

PAGL

PAGL is an acronym for *Peace, Assurance, Gratitude, Love*. The concept of PAGL encapsulates the spiritual qualities we sense when we have caught a glimpse of divine Truth in our contemplative moments, prayer or meditation. Its presence in consciousness signals the timely arrival of whatever goodness, harmony or healthy solution is needed in our material existence. The qualities in PAGL are the Metapsychiatric signs of the Kingdom of God on Earth when the invisible becomes visible.

These four spiritual qualities are palpable aspects of divine Reality which, together with other infinite attributes of God, such as, joy, harmony, wisdom, beauty, order, freedom and mercy, constitute the substance of Cosmic Consciousness. When we can be aware that God — Divine Reality — does exist and is the sole governing, guiding, harmonizing Presence and Power in charge of our lives under all circumstances, regardless of appearances to the contrary, we are in a blessed state of consciousness. The presence of PAGL in our consciousness assures us that whatever issue we have sought to understand is on its way to being healed; its presence substantiates that we are on the "right track" with our lives. We can trust it completely without needing to know what visible form the outcome or next step will take. God is in control. God is always in control. It is only ignorance which obscures this truth from our vision. Resting in PAGL consciousness is what keeps us "in tune" with the One Mind and helps us to listen to Its loving and intelligent messages to us as It guides and animates our everyday lives. Conversely, if there is an absence of PAGL, if we are anxious, apprehensive or hesitant about responding to a certain idea or direction, we are not on the "right track." We must stop, do nothing, and seek to rediscover God's ever-present Presence; we must "retune" our sacred instrument, which is consciousness, so that a right solution can be revealed. Then PAGL can descend like the "dove" of Spirit (Mt. 3:16). PAGL is the supreme good of life; it is an inner knowing, a spiritual good — a nondimensional, yet recognizable, "good" of God. The idea is to learn to live habitually in *PAGL point*, to be continually in a state of grace. This state is synonymous with "spiritual blessedness." Spiritual good is not an abstract because it translates itself into whatever is needed in the material realm and demonstrates itself as the abundance of the kingdom of God in our lives. We do not ever have to ask for anything; we only need to behold the truth-of-being, and let the good reveal itself in our experience. When we are living in the "Land of PAGL," the world is friendly, and we are joyful; we are aware of a conflict-free zone of experience, of an overall well-being, and a liberation from our fantasies; we are aware that we are being lifted out of self-confirmatory preoccupations, gradually transcending interaction thinking and the influences of the Four Horsemen, the Five Gates of Hell and the Devil's Pitchfork. We become more intelligent, alert, creative, generous, loving and useful. When the "Land of PAGL" becomes our dwelling place, we are in a perpetual state of spiritual blessedness, a "Heaven on Earth," and we become interested in taking up residency there.

Dialogue

Dialogue is a joint participation of two or more individuals engaged in a process of shedding light on an issue, problem or experience, in order that the healing Truth may be uncovered.

The dialogic method, established by Socrates, is a foundation stone of Metapsychiatry's guidance and counseling. It is a form of communication (using hermeneutic elucidation[1]) which is entirely different from conversation, chatting, debating, discussing, socializing or expressing opinions. It is an issue-oriented form of communication where the Two Intelligent Questions[2] can be posed and answered, where we can see and question our thoughts and cognitive processes as they reveal themselves as our experiences, where our limitations of knowledge and our restricted mental constructs can be exposed and corrected, where clarification of issues and ideas can occur in a nonpersonal, nonjudgmental and compassionate mental environment, and through which consciousness can be expanded by spiritual wisdom. In dialogue, there are no labels or diagnoses; there is no "should" thinking or right or wrong — just the examination of ideas as to their validity. Seekers engage in a free-flowing and spontaneous exchange of questions and responses, calling on divine wisdom to shine the light of understanding into our individual experiences life issues and global concerns. In the dialogic process, there is no self or other: there is only the presence of Truth. The One Mind will deliver whatever insight or message of truth is needed at that holy instant in order to bring us into alignment with the Perfect Love and One Life of God, which, when realized, can heal our bodies and harmonize the body of our experience. "...Where two or three are gathered in my name, there I am [the Christ Consciousness and Spirit of Truth] in the midst of them" (Mt. 18:20).

---

[1] See page 23 of this book for an explanation.
[2] See page 25 of this book for an explanation.

Spiritual Blessedness

Spiritual blessedness is not a human experience, and it cannot be found in the material world. It is a blissful state of consciousness; it is an awareness of the good of God; it is the fruit of knowing perfect Love; it is a realization of Spiritual Reality; it is real happiness without an opposite. "O taste and see that the Lord is good! Happy is the man who takes refuge in him!" (Ps. 34:8).

This realization of the divine Presence occurs when we turn our thoughts wholeheartedly to God and are no longer impressed by appearances and experiences. The path to spiritual blessedness lies in obeying Principle #1 of Metapsychiatry: "Thou shalt have no other interests before the good of God which is spiritual blessedness." When we are available to divine Mind to touch our consciousness, we are blessed. Spiritual blessedness is the gift of Jesus' beatitude: "Blessed are those who hunger and thirst for righteousness [who have a sincere desire and interest to understand the Truth], for they shall be [ful]filled [existentially]" (Mt. 5:6). Human values and material "things" cannot give us fulfillment; in truth, they contribute to existential frustration. But spiritual blessedness is a state of consciousness which manifests as a frictionless zone of experience, where the quality of life is characterized by PAGL, and where "Everything everywhere is already all right" (Prayer of Beholding), where "All things work together for good" (Ro. 8:28) and where "Yes is good, and no is also good" (Principle #5 of Metapsychiatry). Essentially, what is occurring is that we are seeing the Kingdom of God before us, infusing and pervading the phenomenal world. We are seeing clearly what real life is and know what it is not. Whatever is not spiritual blessedness is not Life — it is the illusion of Life and belongs to the counterfeit world. Our consciousness has been purified sufficiently and reborn of spirit (spiritualized), so that it can recognize "what really is" and partake of It. In this sacred state, there is no fear; there are no persons and no relationships, and consequently we have no interactions. We are just aware that life is really good and harmonious. Everyone is friendly, and all things which are needed appear in time. Once we are living in a spiritualized understanding, there is no longer any need to try to control anything. Conscious of a higher Intelligence and an unconditional, perfect Love, ever-present and always invisibly operating and harmonizing all our affairs, we are blessed. We are free and at peace. "Open thou mine eyes, that I may behold wondrous things out of thy law" (Ps. 119:18). Spiritual blessedness is the realized knowledge of our immortality and the deep uninterrupted sense of PAGL that it bestows on us.

Truth-of-Being

Truth-of-being is Oneness; it is the only "I AM"; it is divine Reality, the One Mind and only Being; it is the perfect, indestructible, eternal Life of God, which is wholly good, and it is the assurance of our nondimensional and inseparable existence in It forever; it is man, the spiritual being and infinite consciousness, which is an individualization and emanation of Infinite Divine Consciousness; it is man, the individuated "I am" of the "I AM" Presence, apart from which there is no life (and we can never be separated from this Presence by any experience, not even the experience of "dying").

The truth-of-being is the "All-in-all." To know God, we must see the truth of ourselves as spiritual beings. "God is spirit: and they that worship him must worship him in spirit and in truth" (Jn. 4:24). Given this understanding, no relationship between God and persons is really ever possible. The word relationship implies separation, and from God there is no separation: "I and my Father [divine Love-Intelligence] are one" (Jn. 10:30). The research of quantum physicist, David Bohm, informs us that, as human beings, "we are separate but not separated," that "the entire universe has to be understood as a single, undivided whole." Metapsychiatry is interested in awakening us to see this wholeness, this holiness: there is no separation between the Divine Being and Its manifestations; there is no separation between Cosmic Consciousness and Its individualizations; there is no life apart from God — not ever — despite appearances in this world to the contrary. Realizing our already existing at-one-ment is the soul's liberation from the illusion experience. "You will know the truth, and the truth [of Being] will make you free" (Jn. 8:32).

The Four Horsemen

The four horsemen are four galloping evils: envy, jealousy, rivalry, malice. These four basic and existentially invalid ways of thinking prevail in human relationships and find their source in comparison thinking (i.e., making comparisons about who has what).

Envy is a desire to have what someone else has, and it is ubiquitous. **Jealousy** is a desire to be what someone else is. **Rivalry** is a desire to be better than someone else; it is preoccupied with what others have or do not have, with winning and not losing in order to be superior; it wants to be right and appear to be more knowledgeable than others, even more spiritually enlightened, and ultimately it wants to be in control. It engages consciously or unconsciously in competition and one-upsmanship. Rivalry and jealousy are present not only in business and community life, but also in most marriages and in family life. **Malice** is ill-will toward another; in malice, the rival wants to destroy the "enemy," the one who has what it is that he wants, in order to win and assert superiority. Maligning another — if only in our thoughts — can have dangerous consequences to our health and well-being because it is hateful and hostile; this malevolent and destructive energy can channel itself into the body and hurt us. We must be alert because even admiration and praise can be "cover-ups" — disguised forms of envy and jealousy. Therefore, envy must be "nipped in the bud" as soon as it is recognized in our consciousness, or it will escalate and eventually manifest harmfully. It is competition that unleashes the four galloping evils, and competing is an existentially invalid idea, based on self and other(s). *The Four Horsemen appear in sequence and are progressive, if not checked.* When any of these evils are allowed to be entertained in consciousness, they destroy the good. They inevitably lead to existential failure, the flipside of success, and can eventually lead to pathogenic problems. The aim of envy, in all its subtle, but poisonous stages, is to annihilate the one it envies, i.e., the rival. One socially acceptable form that this desire to annihilate can take is to ignore the rival — to ignore his or her contributions, talents, unique gifts, intelligence, creativity, knowledge, spirituality, possessions, money, stature, position, physical structure, even youth. The rival dismisses as insignificant what the other has and usually criticizes it, condemns it, ridicules it or misrepresents it. This idea of annihilation can also manifest in less subtle ways such as violence and murder, as we see in the archetypal story of the sibling rivalry between Cain and Abel (Gn. 4). The healing (spiritual counterfact) of comparison thinking can occur as we practice seeing that every individual is at a unique point of evolution, and that "God perfecteth that which concerneth you" (Psalm 138:8). Our passages through this world cannot be compared. "...Each has his own special gift from God, one of one kind and one of another" (I Cor. 7:7). We must each realize our divine potential in our own unique and appropriate ways and really come to understand and appreciate, "God's grace [goodness] is thy sufficiency in all things" (II Cor. 12:9). What another has or does is none of our business and has no effect whatsoever on our ability to realize the limitless, ever-available "good of God" in our own lives. The purpose of our lives is to be "here for God" and to come to know Reality. The Four Horsemen lead us astray, adulterating our purpose. We must all be eventually healed of envy and its destructive presence in our consciousness, or we will never get beyond interpersonal life to realize our individual, divine destiny.

The Five Gates of Hell

The five gates of hell are "doors" through which suffering is invited into our lives. They represent five invalid perspectives on life, five ways in which we engage in self-confirmatory activity which distract us from finding truth. It is helpful to be able to identify these perspectives in ourselves. They are:

sensualism, emotionalism, intellectualism,
materialism, personism / personalism.

The **sensualist** is primarily concerned with the pursuit of physical pleasure and the avoidance of its flipside, pain; he or she is preoccupied with sensations, seeking the good of life in sensory stimuli, whatever titillates the senses, gratifies or indulges us. The **emotionalist** sees life in terms of emotions and moods and lets his or her life be guided by how they feel — lots of "ups and downs." Those who over-emphasize the importance of how they feel tend to cognize reality on the basis of feelings and become very anxious, hedonistic, self-indulgent, and even hypochondriacal. The **intellectual** sees life in terms of the intellect — cherishing information, facts, opinions, knowledge — and engages in calculative thinking; the intellectual wants to be known as knowing and seeks to derive pleasure from the experience of displaying what he or she knows. The **materialist** sees the value of life in material possessions — in having things — in acquiring, collecting, holding onto things, such as status, money, objects or even people. The **personist** is psychologically-minded, seeing life from a horizontal perspective as "self and other;" this individual seeks happiness in interpersonal relationships and interaction experiences / the **personalist** takes things personally and tends to personalize everything — people, things, ideas, attributes, and even ignorance. Each gate has its own specific pathogenicity.

Metapsychiatry is not suggesting the discarding of sensations, emotions, knowledge, thinking processes, possessions or friends. What needs to be overcome is our interest in these things and our attachment to these different experiences. If we look at the Christ, we can ask, "Was Jesus concerned with his feelings or personal relationships? With his mother or the disciples? Was he preoccupied with his possessions, with his wardrobe, or what he would eat? Did he seem worried about money?" No. His interest was focused on the Kingdom of God — the truth-of-being — on understanding the nature of It, seeing It, and expressing It. His interest was focused on revealing man the spiritual being, seeing him solely in the context of Divine Reality. The human race is gradually evolving beyond these "gates of hell" to the transcendent level, where the central issue of life is found to be not in the material realm of interpersonal existence, but in the increased awareness and spiritual discernment of eternal, ascendant values — such as, peace, assurance, gratitude, love, freedom, wisdom, joy, harmony, order, beauty, truth, intelligence — and the manifestation of these divine qualities as the real substance of our lives. "...And the gates of hell shall not prevail against it [the truth]" (Mt. 16:18).

The Devil's Pitchfork

The devil's pitchfork is a three-pronged pitchfork, each prong of which symbolizes a form of hypnotism: seduction, provocation, intimidation. These devilish ways of operating are designed to create a division between human consciousness and divine Reality. It is the aim of these three forms of hypnotism to distract us away, to alienate us, from conscious awareness of God's omniactive Presence and our oneness with It.

Seduction occurs when we are being enticed by those existentially invalid ideas and false values to which we are suggestible and which, therefore, particularly influence us and can lead us astray from living in truth. The serpent (or serpentine idea) which tempted Adam and Eve into believing they could exist without God (Gn. 3) was the original seducer. The serpent suggested to Eve that she needed to reach outside of herself to enhance her life experience, even though everything she could ever need was already in God's perfect "Garden of Eden Consciousness."[1] In this moment, when Adam and Eve, our human prototypes, lost sight of their inseparability from God, the illusion of separation and a world of opposites — of good and evil — was born. It "appeared" as our universal experience. The serpentine thoughts continue to seduce us, as charm, fascination, temptation, sensual gratification, pleasurable experiences, as persuading and coaxing, and as all forms of interpersonal interaction. There are innumerable seductive suggestions in the "sea of mental garbage" which exert a powerful affect over people, hypnotizing all of us into self-confirmatory and harmful ways of thinking, acting and experiencing life. The television, for example, is a persuasive vehicle for propagating illness and, at the same time, selling remedies for the same illness; it also encourages violence and criminal behavior by making what is harmful and destructive appear to be attractive, sexy and exciting, even acceptable. When we are seduced, it clouds our discernment of spiritual values and impairs our vision concerning what is good and righteous and what is real. Gaining immunity to seductive ideas means not to be available to the corrupting influences of this world, but to be more interested in who and what we really are as spiritual and the nature of divine Reality which governs us. **Provocation** occurs when one individual attempts to elicit an irritable reaction in another, to provoke a confrontation or argument; it can come out of a desire for interaction or perhaps vengeance. Pressuring, influencing, convincing, blaming, accusing, "should" thinking, are some of the ways through which provocation operates. The individual who is habitually provoking reveals an interest in friction and a desire for excitement; and the one who is easily provoked or irritated has a tendency to be hypnotized into reacting (justifying, explaining or retaliating) which can lead to contentiousness between the parties. Appreciating peacefulness and harmony, and practicing compassion and "letting be," can help both sides of provocation to overcome it. **Intimidation** is an experience of fearfulness (or it is inducing fear in another). When we are afraid, we feel threatened, powerless and helpless. In the face of a threat, real or imagined, we will either react improperly or be paralyzed into inaction. In either state, we are usually unable to respond intelligently, unable to receive the divine idea we need. Calling on Principle #7 of Metapsychiatry and the "Two Intelligent Questions" will help us understand the experience and learn from it. It is really not other people who make us feel intimidated, but our thoughts about them which do. When we are feeling intimidated, it is important to know that no person ever has control over us, and that our supply and our good do not come from other people, but from God. Our protection and safety lie in the conscious realization of God's all-powerful, ever-present Presence in our lives. This understanding dissolves fear and replaces it with divine assurance. Contemplating Psalm 91 can heal a tendency toward fearfulness.

The devil is a personification of self-confirmatory ideation and, as such, has no power. Each of the prongs in the devil's pitchfork hooks us into some form of interaction experience which adulterates the quality of our lives. In some form or another, each of these prongs has excitement in common. When we are seduced, provoked or intimidated, we are hypnotized. When we are hypnotized, we are asleep — unconscious to the truth-of-being — at the mercy of life in the dream of personhood. This distraction is what leads us to the friction and pain of interaction and reaction, of hurts, anger, mistakes, guilt, blame, suffering and regrets. In order to overcome the devil's pitchfork, we must remain alert. "Be sober, be watchful; because your adversary the devil, prowls around like a roaring lion, seeking someone to devour" (I Pet. 5:8). What is this devil? It is just the ignorance of interaction thinking, seeking to confirm the existence of a separate self. If we can identify and specify the precise nature of the interaction experience to which we are exposed — seduction, provocation or intimidation — we can see it for what it is and refuse it. We must emulate Christ's understanding: "...The prince of this world cometh, and hath nothing [no place] in me" (Jn. 14:30). It requires discipline to turn our attention away from the interaction of being seduced, provoked or intimidated by a person or situation, back to Omniaction and the peace and assurance of God, wherein lies whatever intelligent and necessary response is called for. We must wake up, regain conscious awareness and seek to dwell under all circumstances in the divine ideas of the "Ocean of Love-Intelligence." In this way, we spiritualize our consciousness in order to be immune to the hypnotic suggestions emanating from the serpentine thoughts in the "sea of mental garbage." This means that we take our time to consider a suggestion as to its existential validity before acting on it, that we wait before answering provocative words or gestures until we can answer without anger or not at all, that we turn away from an intimidating situation and pray to see God's all-loving omniactive Presence, keeping us safe under all conditions. Consciousness has the faculty of being a "transcendent observer." Such an observer can recognize the presence of the three prongs of the devil's pitchfork, but it is no longer available to be seduced, provoked or intimidated, influenced or pressured. It has the capacity to be aware but unmoved. We can only learn to live and act from this higher, God-confirmatory perspective when we are aware of our ingrained and habitual patterns of self-confirmatory behavior and can understand them. Seeing which ideas we are most suggestible to, what "pushes our buttons," so to speak, allows the meaning to be recognized and healed, and allows us to stop ourselves from the old ways of interacting. "Resist the devil [refuse the temptation], and he [the devilish thought] will flee from you" (Jas. 4:7).

Phenomenology and Hermeneutics

Metapsychiatry engages in a two-step healing method which is spiritual and centered around a special mode of communication called *hermeneutic elucidation*. The "patient" in this work is always our consciousness and its contents, and the "medicine" is always spiritual truth. Hermeneutics is the science of interpretation, and the word is derived from the Greek, *Hermes + tikos.* Hermes is the god of Greek mythology who served as a messenger of the gods. He is usually depicted with wings on his feet and wings on his helmet, denoting his ability to ascend and descend freely between heaven and earth in order to receive and then impart divine messages. Hermeneutics is therefore identified with *communication* (from *Hermes*) and *shedding light* or making clear (from *tikos);* it is the method by which we can perceive, through the faculty of awareness, some aspect of darkness, in order to allow it to be dissolved by the light and clarity of truth. The hermeneutic approach is present in dialogue and encompasses the clarification of existential issues, spiritual principles, Sesoteric teachings, koans and biblical texts. The hermeneutic form of communication governs the Two Intelligent Questions[1]: In the first step, it looks for the *meaning,* or mental equivalent, of an appearance or phenomenon (called *phenomenological perceptivity)* which involves the faculty of spiritual discernment (or an ability to "interpret" or "see") the main mental preoccupations underlying an individual's mental or physical

> **Blessed be the name**
> **of God — He reveals**
> **deep and mysterious things.**
>
> Dan. 2:20,22

suffering, i.e., the existentially invalid thought currently taking visible form as a troublesome experience, problem or symptom; and, in the second step, it offers an existentially valid principle or some aspect of inspired wisdom (called the *spiritual counterfact)* to shed light on, and thus clarify and correct any error in our thinking, thereby obliterating the darkness of our particular experience. The Two Intelligent Questions illuminate the mental processes which manifest as our problems, so that we can really see them, and then lead us to a more intelligent and spiritually-minded viewpoint about what is good and important, where healing can occur. The "new medicine" seems to be moving toward a similar approach concerning physical problems with its emerging emphasis on the "mind-body connection." It offers visualization techniques, breathing meditations, yogic exercises, all sorts of activities which can be helpful, some more effective than others, whose purpose is to orient the mind away from the unhealthy mental vibrations which are believed to be "causing" the problem and engage it, instead, in healthy activities. However, Metapsychiatry sees no "cause" for our problems and no mind-body "connection." As Dr. Hora has clarified, "The mind and the body are not separate entities: the body is the mind [externalizing] and the mind is the body — in the end, there is only mind." Therefore, Metapsychiatry treats only the contents of consciousness ("mind"), and not the body, in its revolutionary approach to healing. Ultimately, hermeneutic clarification seeks to awaken receptive individuals in order to realize their own divinity and life solely in the context of God.

Some Metapsychiatric Juxtapositions

Metapsychiatry bestows on us a precise vocabulary and a unique method of juxtaposition, in order that we might discover the difference between the finite imperfect world of dreams and the infinite perfect Reality of the enlightened consciousness. The examples offered here demonstrate the way Metapsychiatry contrasts ideas, side by side, to reveal what is truth and what is not. It is hoped that becoming familiar with this method of truth-realization, individuals will be encouraged to engage in the process of juxtaposing ideas so that they can identify if the thoughts they are entertaining are existentially valid or existentially invalid. In this process, harmful thoughts and impure motivations are discerned and exchanged for the pure enlightened ideas which reflect divine Love-Intelligence. In Meta-work, we engage in juxtaposing the material viewpoint with the spiritual viewpoint. We are moving from the Adamic perspective of sense-existence to the soul-existence of the Christ-consciousness, from unawakened human person to awakened spiritual being. And, it is only a spiritual being which can ultimately transcend the world.

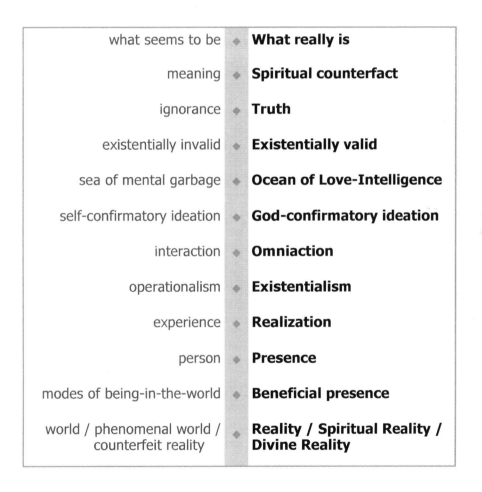

what seems to be	What really is
meaning	**Spiritual counterfact**
ignorance	**Truth**
existentially invalid	**Existentially valid**
sea of mental garbage	**Ocean of Love-Intelligence**
self-confirmatory ideation	**God-confirmatory ideation**
interaction	**Omniaction**
operationalism	**Existentialism**
experience	**Realization**
person	**Presence**
modes of being-in-the-world	**Beneficial presence**
world / phenomenal world / counterfeit reality	**Reality / Spiritual Reality / Divine Reality**

The Two Intelligent Questions

A double doorway at the entrance to the Kingdom of God." — Thomas Hora

"What is the meaning of what seems to be?"	**"What is what really is?"**
What is the specific corresponding thought demonstrating itself as the problem I seem to be having?	*What is the specific aspect of divine Truth that I need to see in order to bring healing or a solution to this situation?*

**A thing can be revealed only through another thing that resists it;
Light cannot reveal itself without darkness, nor good without evil,
nor spirit without matter.**

— Jacob Boehme, 16th century German shoemaker and mystic

Socrates taught that man's purpose is to dedicate his life to the enlightenment of his soul — to seeing the Light — rather than to the pursuit of materialism and the sensory experiences which lead to darkness. Metapsychiatry uses the transitory, material experience (darkness) to reveal the existence of the eternal, nonmaterial divine Reality (Light). It exposes false ideas or lies to enable us to see truth. It accomplishes this holy task through a juxtapositional method, which is the heartbeat of the Metapsychiatric healing process, and which is realized in the "Two Intelligent Questions" (so-called, because they are inspired and lead to intelligent solutions). The "Two Intelligent Questions" underlie the process of "hermeneutic elucidation," offering a uniquely specific approach to liberation from the darkness of ignorance into the light of truth. These questions invite us to examine ideas as to their existential validity by contrasting them: it involves recognition of a specific existentially invalid idea which is present in consciousness (the answer to the first intelligent question) and its dissolution as consciousness is reoriented toward contemplation of a relevant and specific existentially valid idea (which is a spiritual truth and the answer to the second intelligent question). Whenever a student of Metapsychiatry is faced with any problem in life, he or she poses both of these questions, and eventually comes to welcome the answers because they correct and heal the difficulty, even though it can be embarrassing and uncomfortable during the process. Meta-work does not ever engage in cause-and-effect thinking. It is important to understand that we live in an acausal universe. (Physicist Heisenberg's Uncertainty Principle substantiates this basis.) We do not ask what caused something to happen or who or what is to blame for an occurrence. In other words, we never look for "causes" to explain "effects." Instead, we seek *meanings*, acknowledging that thoughts manifest as phenomena. Phenomena, or appearances, can be seen as existentially valid or as existentially invalid, depending on the kind of thought that has been entertained. This dynamic is called the Law of Correspondence or the Law of Attraction. (Principle #7 of Metapsychiatry addresses this law.)

The first intelligent question requires us to find the *meaning* of the situation: the mental equivalent (or corresponding thought) manifesting itself in some visible form as our physical or mental suffering or as a difficult or disturbing experience. The answer to the first intelligent question always reveals a self-confirmatory thought — an existentially invalid thought from the "sea of mental garbage" — which, in whatever form it takes, corresponds to every difficulty we experience. Whatever the nature of this self-confirmatory thought, it will support the lie that we are separate from God — i.e., that we are self-existing persons who are able to live apart from divine Life; it is a thought which hypnotizes us into believing that interaction and the finite world are real, instead of the dreams and illusions that they are. The particular dynamic in this thought must be uncovered and expunged if the difficulty is to be dissolved. (It could be a thought of interaction or of an expectation from a relationship or of resentment, anger, jealousy, rivalry, anxiety, fear, pride, vanity, ambition, self-glorification, self-gratification, self-promotion, "should" thinking, taking things personally, and so forth.) The second intelligent question requires us to look beyond the picture of a problem or symptom and seek to find the truth that can set us free of it. The answer to the second intelligent question, *in juxtaposition to the first*, reveals a *spiritual truth* or *insight*, a *divine law* or *principle*, which we call the *spiritual counterfact*. This *spiritual counterfact* substantiates in some specific and helpful way that we are emanations of God, completely dependent on God for everything in our lives, that there is no separation between divine Life and Its manifestations, and that this Life, which is God, is wholly good, perfectly loving and supremely intelligent under all conditions. This existentially valid, God-confirmatory understanding has power to correct and, thus, erase the *meaning* or impure thought which is manifesting as our problem, experience or symptom. In the moment that we realize that needed aspect of Truth, and catch a glimpse of our already-existing wholeness (holiness), we can be healed. (This faculty of beholding was most likely the secret of Jesus' healing power. He was able to separate the impure thought from the individual demonstrating it, and behold the hidden wholeness of Perfect Life right where the fragmentation of sickness seemed to be.) When any form of ignorance, such as a fantasy or false belief, a self-serving value system or deluded idea about who and what we are, and the purpose of our life, is corrected, the phenomenon which this thought was demonstrating is also corrected: the light of Truth dispels the darkness of an ignorant thought (hermeneutic elucidation). When the energy of the (inner) thought is dispelled, its (outer) visible form will also disappear. Healing can be instantaneous or gradual, depending on our receptivity and ability to grasp the spiritual idea we need. Sometimes we have to repeat the process several times before we are really able to integrate the truth; but each time we put the method to the test, we are consciously expanding into Truth.

By juxtaposing aspects of the material experience ("what seems to be") with the nonmaterial, spiritual truth-of-being ("what really is"), we are able to separate the ideas of illusion from the ideas of Reality. Experiencing what is not (real, good or emanating from the Mind of God) — such as, illness, deprivation, discord, sadness, mistakes, disappointment, anger — can have value: the pain of it drives us to move out of our suffering into spiritual understanding. Therefore, our suffering has a purpose — it can force us to seek an alternative, a valid alternative, which is always spiritual. The nature of consciousness is that it becomes cognizant of itself as an entity of awareness in juxtaposition to a lie. As Dr. Hora has said: "Lies, therefore, can be useful." Experiencing matter, the body, dimensionality, time, space and limitations can force us to go beyond this imperfect world of appearances and experiences in order to uncover perfect Reality which is nonmaterial, incorporeal, nondimensional, timeless and infinite, the realm of consciousness, the truth-of-being. This discovery tells us what we really are and gives new meaning and purpose to existence. Most importantly, it validates itself in our existence by dissolving our suffering and problems once the meaning has been discerned and corrected by the truth. (We call this "proof" the Principle of Existential Validation.) In the realm of the Two Intelligent Questions, we have "overcome the world" and its "tribulations" (Jn. 16:33) and entered into another dimension of reality, one which is characterized by harmony, understanding, peace, assurance, gratitude and love. One of the healing values of the Two Intelligent Questions is that it does not allow us to exchange one dream for another, but instead they shift us out of the dream into the Truth that transforms.

Light cannot reveal itself without darkness,

Nor spirit without matter or physicality,

Nor Infiniteness without finiteness,

Nor a healing without a symptom of disease or disharmony,

Nor a blessing without the experience of need or difficulty,

Nor abundance and generosity without lack,

Nor a loving resolution or correction without a problem or mistake,

Nor a miracle without an insurmountable challenge or obstacle,
Nor the power of God without the limitation of human existence.

Editor's note: It can be helpful to use the process of alchemy as an analogy to understand the Two Intelligent Questions because both processes involve transmutation or a change across substances. Just as alchemy converts base metal into gold, the Two Intelligent Questions convert the substance of our consciousness from base and dark human thoughts to pure and illumined spiritual ideas. Thus, whenever a symptom or experience is converted into its constituent thought (its meaning) and that invalid thought is replaced with spiritual understanding (its spiritual counterfact), the meaning is consumed and the phenomenon can be transformed. It is the activity of Truth translating across substances, conditions, situations, forms.

The Juxtapositional Method

What Seems to Be

What seems to be is the visible, material, phenomenal world, the world of symbolic structures, of cause-and-effect thinking, of dualistic thinking — i.e., opposites — and of pictures, dreams and fantasies; it is the illusion of life in personhood, the collective dream of experiential life, the hologram.

Whatever seems to be — whether it is steel or gold or diamonds or flesh or bones — is not really substance. Spirit is the substance of everything that is real, of everything that really is. It is difficult to comprehend that the tangible is insubstantial, and the intangible is substantial (of real substance), but it can be gradually realized through the awakened faculty of spiritual discernment. Quantum physics sees the nature of the universe as holographic — a realm of infinite potentialities and frequencies underlying an illusion of concreteness; it proposes that we are living in a transparent universe and that material structures are not at all what they seem to be. Neurological surgeon and scientist, Karl Pribram, who did extensive research on the brain, postulated that the brain is a hologram, explaining a holographic universe, a kind of lens interpreting reality and the universe as material and finite. Since our brains are universally conditioned by the prevailing culture and by our common collective assumptions, and since we see with our thoughts, we interpret what we see in a similar way. The mystics teach us that when we are spiritually illumined, we can transcend the brain's holographic picture of reality to see what ordinary people cannot see and discern divine Reality. "What seems to be," therefore, is all that is temporal, finite, impermanent and not real — the dimensional world of matter and of "form and formlessness." It is a dream. The world of "what seems to be" is inhabited by seemingly self-existent persons, living apart from God, with ego identities and separate minds and wills of their own (through which they try to have a relationship with God, which will never bring the desired understanding); this world is constituted of the human experiences of pleasure and pain, and of the suffering, aging and death of these persons. This concrete world of appearances is made up of thoughts — self-confirmatory ideation and interaction thinking — manifesting in visible form. All phenomena are externalizations of thoughts and thought-processes. As physicist-astronomer, Sir Arthur Eddington said, "The stuff of the world is mind-stuff." However, this material experience is useful as a counterpoint to lead us to discover the invisible, nonmaterial, eternal divine Reality and our already-existing place in It, which is "what really is." "Therefore, we look not at the things which are seen, but at the things which are unseen; for the things which are seen are temporal, and the things which are unseen are eternal" (II Cor. 4:18).

> Nothing is as it seems to be and neither is it otherwise.
> — Zen koan

What really is consists of the "unseen and eternal," nondual realm of Spirit — the infinite domain of God which is operating everywhere always — and whose existence substantiates man's true identity as spiritual. It is a synonym for divine Reality, for God's perfect Universe of nondual Good, for perfect Love and supreme Intelligence, for the divine Presence and Omniaction, for the truth-of-being; its substance is nonmaterial, incorporeal, nondimensional, indestructible, everlasting Life, and, as an individualization of It, we are each already dwelling in this sacred and immortal Life — regardless of appearances to the contrary and whether we know it or not.

We are distracted, absorbed and overwhelmed by the apparently concrete picture of the phenomenal world and by our experiences in it. We cannot become aware of "what really is" as perfect Life until we begin to wake up from the dream of "what seems to be" real, and our eyes are opened. "What really is" reveals itself in juxtaposition to "what seems to be" when a spiritual realization or insight occurs in consciousness, which often happens when we are suffering or struggling through a problem or a symptom and reach beyond our limited human understanding for a transcendent solution to the situation we are experiencing. In this instance, Reality can enter and fill our receptivity, and It becomes "real" to us: "what seems to be" is obliterated. The Bible says, "When the perfect [understanding] will come, the imperfect [situation] will disappear" (I Cor. 13:10). This dynamic explains what happens when healings occur, problems dissolve, corrections and adjustments take place and harmonizing solutions present themselves in our human affairs. "The understanding of what really is abolishes all that seems to be" (Principle #10 of Metapsychiatry). "What really is" is ours for the seeking — we do not have to earn it, deserve it, beg, bargain or plead for it. It already is, and it is infusing the world of "what seems to be." All that is needed is for us to see it. Seeing "what really is" requires the awakened faculty of spiritual discernment and the ability to break whatever picture is before us and transcend it. On the way to uncovering "what really is," it can be helpful to "bracket,"[1] to "mind-fast," to pray and meditate. This reorientation of consciousness is what invites spiritual blessedness into our lives.

> **IS-ness is our business.**
>
> — *Thomas Hora*

---

[1] The practice of "bracketing" and "mind-fasting" means that we put any distracting or disturbing thoughts aside in "brackets," and we "fast" from thinking about them, while we seek to see the presence of God.

Meaning[1]

Meaning is the mental equivalent of a phenomenon and the answer to the first of the Two Intelligent Questions; it is always an existentially invalid and self-confirmatory thought, which finds its origin in the "sea of mental garbage."

A meaning is not to be confused with a cause. Behind every problem, difficult experience, disturbance, unhealthy behavior, harmful activity, symptom, pain or disease, there is a constituent, or corresponding, thought which is manifesting itself. This means that every appearance is a thought which has taken shape. The appearance, or phenomenon, is a "message" alerting us to some form of ignorance in our consciousness, which can be spiritually discerned through phenomenological perceptivity, and can then be healed after it is replaced by some aspect of spiritual understanding. (The specific aspect of healing spiritual truth that is needed is uncovered when we pose the second of the Two Intelligent Questions.) Discerning meanings occurs as inspired and spontaneous insights "obtaining" in consciousness and is primary in the Meta-therapeutic process. Without accurately identifying the particular existentially invalid thought we are entertaining, we cannot really purify the contents of consciousness. There is a process of alchemy inherent in the Two Intelligent Questions. Locating the meaning of a phenomenon activates this process so it can begin to work; then,

> An unexamined life
> is a life not worth living.
>
> — *Socrates*

the phenomenon, which has been converted back into the energy of its mental equivalent, can be transformed by the energy of truth (the spiritual counterfact) at its source. To make pure gold, the alchemists of the Middle Ages began their process with base metal; similarly, in order for a consciousness to become illumined, Metapsychiatry begins its process with the meaning. Discovering the meaning of a phenomenon requires complete openness of mind — having no preconceived ideas or assumptions about it. A meaning is usually embarrassing, often disconcerting, and can be painful to recognize. We do not like to admit to ignorance, to not knowing, to a mistaken or destructive idea. But without recognizing the presence of a particular self-confirmatory or interaction thought in consciousness, we will probably continue to invite troublesome or painful experiences into our lives, repeating the same patterns over and over again (which Metapsychiatry identifies as "eternal damnation"). Blaming others, being resentful or angry, or harboring "should" thoughts, we will never understand that there is a correspondence between our thoughts and our experiences. (Metapsychiatry calls this dynamic The Law of Correspondence.) Meanings are always thoughts which come out of the "sea of mental garbage." Without awareness of their presence in consciousness, we are, as Dr. Hora used to say, "just sitting ducks in the devil's shooting gallery." It is by identifying meanings that consciousness is gradually cleansed of the world's mental pollution. We are constantly exposed to suggestions which flood our consciousness with false values and mistaken ideas. Prayer and meditation wash consciousness and fill us with wholesome ideas.

---

[1] See footnote on page 25.

Spiritual counterfact is a divinely inspired idea and the answer to the second of the Two Intelligent Questions; it is always an existentially valid, God-confirmatory thought, which finds its origin in the "Ocean of Love-Intelligence," and which replaces an existentially invalid, self-confirmatory idea, thereby pointing us to healing and transformation; it is a specific spiritual value, divine principle or spontaneously received insight which, through the hermeneutic process of elucidation (shedding light), clarifies the truth for our particular situation and, thereby, brings us into meaningful contact with divine Reality when we can realize it.

When a new message is "recorded" in consciousness, just as with a tape recorder, it will supersede the old message; in other words, the old invalid message ("meaning") is erased by the presence of a new, healing and transforming message of truth (which we call the "spiritual counterfact").

> A new heart I will give you,
> and a new spirit
> I will put within you.
> — Ex. 36:26

The alchemic process of the Two Intelligent Questions is now complete, allowing a change to occur. Thus, it is important not to wallow in a meaning once it has been discerned. We must shift our interest to what is existentially valid, reorienting consciousness toward what God is and what we really are. Concentrating on the healing message is what allows us to be healed. The counterfact, therefore, when sincerely contemplated and understood, can dissolve the presence of the specific meaning which is taking form as a trouble, problem, difficult experience, symptom or distortion. At this point, the problem or symptom can disappear, i.e., be resolved or healed. Without the presence of the invalid thought, the invalid phenomenon cannot remain. This dynamic is the way that consciousness is gradually spiritualized. "And we all, with unveiled face, beholding the glory of the Lord, are being changed into his likeness from one degree of glory to another" (II Cor. 3:18).

---

[1] An example of this two-step therapeutic process:

Question: What is the *meaning* of ("what seems to be") my headache?

Answer: The *meaning* of my headache is discerned to be a thought of resentment, due to a "should" thought, which is resounding in my head.

Question: What is ("what really is") the *spiritual counterfact*?

Answer: What really is, is Principle #2 of Metapsychiatry. (See Page 62.) Realizing the truth of this principle can heal my willful insistence that another "should" act in a certain way, help me to acknowledge that every individual is at a unique point of evolution, and enable me to turn away from ruminating about what "should" or "should not" be. Instead, what is needed is to practice compassion ("understanding the lack of understanding") and forgiveness ("to give up blaming"), and turn attention to being "here for God." (See page 54.) The headache can now disappear because the existentially invalid thought which was manifesting has been corrected and dissolved. There is no longer the thought-energy present in consciousness to transmute into the symptom.

Ignorance is the ignoring of that which is available to be known. Its etymology (from Latin, ignorantia, lack of knowledge, not knowing) informs us that all our suffering finds its source in not knowing — not knowing of the existence of the good of God and Its immutable spiritual laws and principles — and not ever in any personal error. Ignorance is darkness, and darkness is nothing — in the end, it is just the absence of light. When we are "ignoring what is available to be known," the good of God is not available to us — God's value system cannot help us. We cannot benefit from the presence of God when we are interested in and distracted by what is not existentially valid.

Ignorance belongs to the illusory phenomenal world. In the phenomenal world, there are endless manifestations of ignorance: ignorance is the contents of the "sea of mental garbage" — the source of all existentially invalid thoughts — of self-confirmatory ideation and interaction, of operationalism and experiences and of the belief in personhood and relationship-thinking; it governs the world of "what seems to be." Ignorance, in some of its guises, is described in the Four Horsemen, the Five Gates of Hell, and the three prongs of the Devil's Pitchfork. These manifestations of ignorance result in confusion, problems, illness and every kind of suffering; they also include the universal tendency to blame or feel guilty, which only serves to increase our sense of personal selfhood and personal culpability. Admitting to ignorance absolves those tendencies, but this can be difficult for us, depending on whether we are "positive ignorants" or "negative ignorants." (A "positive ignorant" thinks he knows but does not know — a "negative ignorant" knows he does not know, and is, therefore, the more easily redeemed.) The "negative ignorant" is summed up

> Ignorance is not bliss.
>
> — *Thomas Hora*

in Socrates' words: "I know that I do not know anything." And the "positive ignorant" could be summed up in Mark Twain's words: "It ain't what you don't know that gets you into trouble — it's what you think you know that ain't so." Not knowing the truth, and being distracted by the apparent importance of this world and all its facts, statistics, history and collective experiences, leaves us living in the dark and keeps us asleep and unable to see it. Judging by appearances and experiences, which are sensory based, leads most of mankind to make erroneous assumptions and conclusions about the nature of existence. Self-confirmatory strivings keep us in a state of ignorance by inducing us to ignore "what really is." Ignorance is not a person, and it is not personal. If offended or hurt by it, we must learn to separate the offense (offensive thought) from the offender (an "image" and "likeness" of God). Only in this way can we practice forgiveness and be forgiven — giving up blaming ourselves or another. Ignorance must always be depersonalized even when it manifests as sin, guilt or, in its most hostile, malicious and destructive form, as evil, personified as the very devil. Evil is the outpicturing of dark, twisted and corrupt thoughts polluting the planet's race consciousness since the beginning of time. It can take the form of violence, war, terrorism, tornadoes, cyclones, floods, firestorms, and the like. The phenomena of ignorance falsify the true nature of divine Reality. Evil is godlessness — it is an extreme form of ignorance, a perversion of Truth, and not an autonomous power which militates against good. Mistakes, lies, dishonesty adulterate the truth-of-being. Our undeveloped, unawakened cognitive abilities and our universal existential miseducation (basing life on a mistaken formula, like $2 + 2 = 5$) obfuscate the knowledge available to be known, and keep our attention away from seeing the light of Truth. Jesus said, "You do err, not knowing the scriptures, nor the power of God" (Mt. 22:29). The healing remedy for ignorance is spiritual knowledge. As we replace our ignorant, misdirected interests with relevant truths, and are willing to rearrange our lives to conform to what is healthy and intelligent, there will be a gradual "melt-down" of the ignorance. But we can only be redeemed from a state of darkness when we are willing to admit to not knowing what we did not know — that we were ignorant.

Truth

Truth is that which IS; it is a valid statement about "what really is;" it is knowing our true identity as spiritual beings and God as the only Power and Presence; it is a synonym for God; it is the light of right knowledge; it is the truth-of-being; it is the One; it is Existence, Consciousness, the Absolute — the Ultimate Reality in which we "live and move and have our being" eternally: It is the only real transformative Power in the universe — It can move through all substances. Truth is not visible, yet it can be clearly seen.

Truth is the unseen, nondimensional Power that is recognizable as it clarifies, corrects, heals, liberates and imparts harmony into human life. Truth operates as divine laws, spiritual values and attributes, and It expresses immutable, indestructible principles of good, such as, unconditional perfect Love and supreme Intelligence. Truth is that God is the only Being, the One Mind, One Life, only Power and Presence in the Universe, and every individual is but one of Its infinite individualizations.

> There is no one here but
> God.
> — *Thomas Hora*

Truth is that God is the only I AM. Truth expresses itself as inspired ideas, as wisdom and love, as compassion, harmony, creativity and goodness. "When the Spirit of truth comes, it will guide you into all the truth" (Jn. 16:13). These words point to the truth that truth, once discerned and realized, expands itself without any effort on our part. All that is needed is interest and humility; and then truth dawns on us by grace of God. And it keeps on dawning on us as our interest increases. The Buddha was asked, "How can we know Truth?" He replied: "You can know Truth because Truth works." Only the light of spiritual truth has power to eradicate the darkness of not knowing and transform us — all condemnation of man or woman disappears, all sin, guilt and evil are consumed. "And you shall know the truth, and the truth shall make you free" (Jn. 8:32).

Metapsychiatry does not label thoughts judgmentally as right or wrong, as good or bad, as positive or negative, but defines them according to the way they manifest and thereby validate themselves in our existence. It distinguishes between two kinds of thoughts: existentially invalid and existentially valid. Before enlightenment is attained, our consciousness is manifesting a mixture of valid and invalid thoughts. Our experiences mirror our thoughts back to us and are helpful in alerting us as to which kinds of thoughts we are entertaining, so that we can continue to cleanse consciousness of the unwanted thoughts.

Existentially Invalid

Existentially invalid describes those ideas, thoughts, concepts, values, notions, beliefs, opinions, assumptions and so-called facts, which belong to the dimensional world of "what seems to be" and which do not bear "good fruit": they do not heal us, liberate us or enhance the quality of our existence and well-being — they are ultimately pathogenic — and their presence in consciousness interferes with the fulfillment of our divine potential.

Existentially invalid thoughts are impure and emanate from the "sea of mental garbage," and they encompass virtually every kind of self-confirmatory and interaction thought since the beginning of time — envy, jealousy, rivalry, malice (the Four Horseman, which are all forms of comparison thinking), greed, fear, anger, blame, criticism, guilt, self-promotion, self-glorification, self-deprecation, vanity, pride, ambition, "should" thinking, influencing, all thoughts coming out of sensualism, emotionalism, materialism, intellectualism and personalism (the Five Gates of Hell), seduction, intimidation, provocation (the three prongs of the Devil's Pitchfork), and judging by appearances and experiences.

> **Everything depends upon the thoughts we entertain.**
> — *Thomas Hora*

The answer to the first of the Two Intelligent Questions is always existentially invalid and self-confirmatory in nature, in other words, a "garbage thought," and is what gets us into a quagmire of false beliefs which, in turn, manifest as our problems, difficulties and sicknesses. Invalid thoughts are designed by ignorance to perpetuate the illusion of separation; they are the substance of the phenomenal world and are ultimately seen to be impermanent and, therefore, not real. Invalid thoughts tend to transmute themselves into our existence as invalid phenomena. Invalid phenomena distract us from seeing the truth-of-being and falsify the true nature of divine Reality.

Existentially valid describes those ideas, thoughts, concepts or values of wisdom and truth, which belong to the nondimensional realm of "what really is" and which bear "good fruit": they heal us, liberate us and enhance the quality of our existence and well-being — they are always health-promoting — and are what enable us to fulfill our indwelling divine potential.

Existentially valid thoughts are pure and emanate from the "Ocean of Love-Intelligence" (the divine Mind) and they encompass spiritual qualities and values, inspired wisdom and love, creative and intelligent ideas and divine principles. The answer to the second of the Two Intelligent Questions is always existentially valid and God-confirmatory in nature; understanding a spiritual truth is what sets us free from a harmful, mistaken perception (or mistaken "formula") and allows for its beneficial correction. Valid thoughts are expressions of nondimensional Reality, which substantiate the truth of One, and by virtue of their Source can obliterate any lie circulating in the dimensional world. Valid thoughts, therefore, are permanent and real, i.e., eternal and inviolable truths.

> **The earth is full of the goodness of the lord.**
>
> — *Ps. 35:5*

Valid thoughts tend to transmute themselves into our existence as valid phenomena and, thus, verify the true nature of divine Reality. The Principle of Existential Validation, "Ye shall know them by their fruits" (Mt. 7:16), informs us of the validity or invalidity of a thought by the way in which it manifests as our experience.

Sea of mental garbage is a metaphor to describe the collective mental climate of the phenomenal world with all its distortions of Truth; it is the sum total of all existentially invalid thoughts of the human race since the beginning of time; it is the repository of all harmful and destructive ideas which are perceived by the senses and manifest as our pain and suffering, difficulties and sorrows; it is every lie about who and what we are and what our purpose is; in other words, its content is the darkness of ignorant ideas. The "sea of mental garbage" is synonymous with such terms as collective consciousness, personal mind, "carnal mind," illusion, noosphere, samsara and maya (which translates from the Sanskrit as "that which is not").

The mental climate in which we experience our daily lives is determined by the contents of our own consciousness, by the prevailing thoughts of our culture, of the people around us, of the media, newspapers and internet, of our friends and enemies and what they are thinking about us — what they are all communicating, consciously and unconsciously, overtly, covertly and subliminally to us. Metapsychiatry helps us to recognize the different manifestations of this mental garbage with specific terms such as self-confirmatory ideation and interaction thinking, as dualistic thinking,

> For [it] is a liar
> and the father of it.
> — *Jn. 8:44*

"should" thinking, as "judging by appearance" and experience, the Five Gates of Hell, the Four Horsemen, the Devil's Pitchfork. The total of all these stimuli comes to us through our sensory apparatus. It is important to recognize that *every* garbage thought potentiates the illusion of separation, however subtle, that *every* thought in this cesspool encourages and supports self-confirmatory ideation and interaction thinking, urging us in one invalid direction after another. Everything we humanly perceive, including our ideas of ourselves, is a projection of this polluted collective "mind." What God has created is perfect; but ignorance has misinterpreted and distorted the good ideas of God. (An example of a distortion of truth would be to examine the way love is understood and misunderstood.) Instead of being a pure, conscious transparency to reveal the attributes of God, man has twisted divine ideas and uses them to glorify and gratify himself which, in turn, gives him a false sense of identity — confirming the illusory belief that his life has an existence apart from God, that he is an autonomous, finite person with his own ideas, living under his own steam in a material realm, and in control of his experiences. Garbage thoughts are designed to influence us to believe in separate minds and separate wills and separate lives outside of the One Mind. It is these distortions of truth, and its dreams and fantasies, which constitute the "sea of mental garbage," keeping us asleep and confused, unable to see our already-existing oneness and divine purpose.

Ocean of Love-Intelligence is a Metapsychiatric "fantasy" which is a descriptive metaphor for the infinite, divine Source out of which flow all intelligent, useful, loving, inspired and creative ideas, all spiritual qualities, values and divine laws, and, therefore, all existentially valid thoughts; Its contents are filled with the light of Truth and manifest as our good, giving clarity to who and what we are and helping us to see and know our divine purpose; It is a synonym for the dwelling place of God.

In the context of this metaphor, awakened man can see himself as a wave, as an individualized aspect of the Ocean, yet always one with it. There is no separation between the wave and the ocean — the wave is made of the same substance as the ocean, and it has no life apart from or without the ocean — the wave is undivided from the ocean. This Ocean permeates us, surrounds us, supports us, maintains us, animates us, fills us, protects us, washes over us, lives through us, and floods consciousness with Its Love and Intelligence and insights of Truth: Its content is God-confirmatory, existentially valid ideation, which is always good without an opposite; It is healing and uplifting, inspiring, creative, life-affirming and life-enhancing. Conscious recognition of the existence of this Ocean and immersion in It will allow us to realize at-one-ment and our divine purpose to reveal God. "The spiritual laws of Life are always operating. We can lean on them as we lean on the buoyancy of water" (Thomas Hora).[1]

> How lovely is thy dwelling place,
> O Lord of Hosts!
>
> — Ps. 84:1

---

[1] Editor's note: Professor of physics, John Hagelin, Ph.D., author and speaker on Consciousness and Superstring Unified Field Theory, is now calling the "Unified Field" an "Ocean of Existence" at the basis of everything, of mind and matter. "At the deepest possible level, we discover one Unified Ocean — of which you are a wave and I am a wave — just different [unique] vibrational frequencies of this One Universal Field." He describes the "Ocean" as a "nonmaterial Field," a "universal Field of Consciousness," and "everything — planets, people, animals and plants — are just 'waves' of vibration, emanating from this underlying unified or superstring Field, really united [at one] at the core of Being." He goes on to say, "There is only One Consciousness," and that even though we experience "life" as "you and me," as individualized, "at the core there is only One. Knowing this is enlightenment." He describes the Field as "pure intelligence" because, at its basis, "the universe is not a material universe or inert — it is alert, alive and conscious. Its existence informs us that we are really living in a thought universe...and we create our own realities." The language of Metapsychiatry has long offered us a vocabulary to point us to eternal truths in order to help us see the Infinite. And, now, some quantum physicists are, most remarkably, echoing that same extraordinary vocabulary.

The following juxtaposition of terms informs us that ideas are nonpersonal. No person is personally responsible for anything that happens. We are not in control of our lives — ideas are. We do not even make decisions — ideas do. However, we can make choices — we choose certain ideas over others, and it is the ideas we choose that urge us in one direction or another and, thus, determine our experiences and the quality of our lives — individually and globally. Metapsychiatry identifies two pools of ideation whose ideas we entertain. This term, ideation, simply stated, means a persistent dwelling in certain ideas and, thus, being influenced by them. The term, ideation, is quite intentionally offered to depersonalize the source of all thoughts; remembering that it is the nature of consciousness to receive thoughts (thoughts "obtain") — not to generate or produce them — we can neither take credit for the spiritual, beneficial, healing ideas which reach us from the Mind of God, nor are we blameworthy for the ignorant, harmful, pathogenic ideas which assail us from the world's garbage heap. When we are awakened to be able to differentiate between what kinds of thoughts we are entertaining, we become "gatekeepers of consciousness," responsible for the contents of our consciousness, responsible for the thoughts which we allow to gain entry. It is the faculty of "spiritual discernment" which enables us to become "stewards of consciousness" and, thereby, to have "dominion over all the earth" (Gn. 1:26-27), over earthly thoughts and worldly values. Metapsychiatry distinguishes between the two ideations in which we can choose to dwell as self-confirmatory ideation or God-confirmatory ideation. Consciousness is available to entertain thoughts from either of these two pools of ideation.

Self-Confirmatory Ideation

Self-confirmatory ideation is constituted of ignorant ideas which constantly seek to reassure us that we really do exist as independent, self-existent, self-propelled persons — in other words, it is persistent thinking about oneself in the infinite variety of ways which tempt us to confirm the lie of separation, the lie of an autonomous ego-identity, living a finite life in a material realm; self-confirmatory ideas keep us asleep.

There is one essential, existentially invalid idea (one mistaken "formula"), out of which all the varieties find their source: it is the mistaken idea that there is separation between God and man/woman, the spiritual being, which has led us to believe that we are autonomous and can exist apart from Being Itself. This is a lie, regardless of appearances to the contrary, and it is designed to support the illusion of personhood and separation and hypnotize us continually away from knowing Perfect Life. This lie leads us to a misdirected habit of fearfully contemplating our condition in life and to an exaggerated self-concern. Self-confirmatory ideation and interaction thinking are the source of all our human suffering; they go together and emanate from the "sea of mental garbage."

The term, *ideation*, is intentionally used by Metapsychiatry to help us see that all self-confirmatory ideas emanate from a universal pool or repository of ignorant ideas and not from any person — there is nothing personal about them. (Thoughts "obtain" — are received — in consciousness: we entertain thoughts, but we are not responsible for producing them. We only think that we think. A thought is a unit of energy, and is seeking a consciousness which will receive it. We receive those thoughts to which we are most suggestible, according to what we cherish, hate or fear, until such time as we gain immunity to them through a spiritualized consciousness.) This term, ideation, compassionately depersonalizes all blame and guilt, sorrows and grievances, discord and disease, mistakes and problems. It is always existentially invalid thoughts which manifest as our suffering, and it is our unconsciousness about what kinds of thoughts we are attracting which is the source of our human tribulations. The term self-confirmatory ideation replaces the psychological term, ego. Metapsychiatry defines ego as "the mental picture we have of ourselves which we carry around with us wherever we go": it is the "I" that we dream that we are, the "thinker" and the "doer" that we dream that we are, and it is summed up in the self-confirmatory thought, "I want." Metapsychiatry does not speak of the ego or the ego-identity because the term encourages the illusory belief that we are persons with egos, with a form-identity, which must be resisted or enhanced or regarded as real. Instead, Metapsychiatry places the emphasis on thoughts and the contents of our consciousness as the nonpersonal focal point. As the contents of consciousness are gradually cleansed, the so-called ego — the "thinker" and "doer" — is dissolved.

Confirming the "self" comes out of the human instinct for self-preservation. This urge finds its genesis in the collective fear of non-being, what Heidegger called the "dread of nothingness." "The fear of non-being is a universal human experience which needs to be individually confronted," said Dr. Hora. This existential fear or "dread" is a deep, undefined fear that the person we are is not real, that we might not really be here, that we are really no-thing. It is this fear of being nothing which we try to combat through self-confirmation. This fear leads us to cling to our belief that we really do exist as persons, and unconsciously we look for every way to confirm and promote ourselves as persons in order to overcome the fear. We have to come, eventually, to see how this fear drives us to seek to escape the feeling of being insignificant, ignored, abandoned, lonely, and destined for a death which means oblivion. The built-in ignorance of the human condition works to impress upon us, at every opportunity, that our finiteness and the material experience are absolutely real, possibly all there is, and we have to be a "somebody." Unfortunately, this dynamic has the effect of further deluding us and keeping us stuck and unable to overcome the illusion of personhood. However, Hora clarifies, "What we are afraid of is an impossibility...in order for an individual to cease being, God would have to be destroyed. God is our Being, and we are inseparable from God." Therefore, as Dr. Hora goes on to conclude, "Non-being is an

> We are neither something nor nothing —
> we are fullness of Being.
> — *Thomas Hora*

impossibility." The self is not real; there are no persons anywhere; this world is a shadow reality. "We are neither something nor nothing – we are fullness of Being" (Thomas Hora). This dread of no-thing-ness can only be dissolved through spiritual knowledge. As we gradually come to recognize our divine nature as existing beyond appearances, we realize ourselves to be eternally safe in God; we are each an eternal, indestructible consciousness, and this world is just a dream in the body, a dream of relationships, interactions and material existence.

Self-confirmatory thoughts keep us entangled in interpersonal physical life, suffering from the past, agonizing in the present, and anxious about the future; they keep us in "survival" mode, living in the fantasies and expectations of the ego-life, restricted by the finite, grasping for the transient, the illusive, the impermanent, never fulfilled. The Sufi poet, Rumi, aptly sums up the confusion in which self-confirmatory ideation puts us: "I have spent my time stringing and unstringing my instrument, while the song I came to sing remains unsung." The kinds of self-confirmatory thoughts which are circulating "to and fro upon the earth...up and down on it" (Job 1:7), and which ensnare us, are innumerable. They can be identified only in broad strokes, as the vain, proud, ambitious thoughts we entertain, as the guilty, blaming, resentful, impatient, retaliatory, argumentative, confrontational, angry, accusatory, judging, condemnatory, critical, fearful thoughts we entertain, as the envious, rivalrous and competitive thoughts we entertain, as the wanting and not wanting, as the "shoulds" and "should nots," as the greed and materialism that so prevail in our culture, as self-interest and self-promotion, as excitement and seriousness, as our fantasies and dreams about ourselves, as desires for attention, approval, admiration, praise, recognition, fame and personal influence, and as our bloating tendencies toward self-glorification, self-gratification and self-importance. In short, it is any idea whatsoever which magnifies the erroneous idea of separation and a belief in personal power and persuades us away from seeing the truth-of-being. Trying to live as persons, viewing life as interpersonal and material and not as spiritual, invites us to attract the ideas which support our false "formula." We are taught universally that

> Nothingness,
> in contrast to all that seems
> to be, is the veil of Being.
> — *Heidegger*

we are persons, and we are firmly attached to that self-identity. Along with it, we are attached to our personalities, personal histories, genealogies, and all the souvenirs of the fiction of personhood. Therefore, self-confirmatory ideas can gain entry into any consciousness which sees life as a person, separate and apart from God. Self-confirmatory thinking leads to a Godless existence and, ultimately, to self-destruction. "Self-confirmation is self-destruction; self-destruction is self-confirmation" (Thomas Hora). Even destroying ourselves is "confirming" ourselves because it means we believe that there is an independent self over which we have control. In a self-confirmatory consciousness, there is only "self and other." However, self-confirmation can be an issue for clarification — it serves Truth because the troubles it invites can drive us to discover the One Perfect Life and our already-existing place in It. Becoming aware of God-confirmatory ideation is the way out of any idea which endeavors to hypnotize us into believing in a separate and dimensional, autonomous self or a mind or existence apart from God, the One Mind, the One Life, the Perfect Spiritual Reality. As we replace self-confirmatory thoughts with God-confirmatory thoughts, our consciousness is gradually cleansed and awakened to see a Higher Reality. "Empty and be full" (Zen koan).

God-Confirmatory Ideation

God-confirmatory ideation is constituted of spiritual ideas which support and awaken us to see our already-existing oneness with the divine Mind — in other words, in being attentive to thoughts of truth and love and joy and beauty and goodness and peace and harmony and wisdom, "obtaining" (being received) in consciousness, which constantly affirm us as nondimensional and incorporeal consciousness and the presence of God as the only Reality, the only Mind and Power, the Infinite Life from which we are eternally inseparable.

In this mental environment, we are living in God-Consciousness and not in the realm of persons or in interpersonal life in a finite world. God-confirmatory thoughts emanate from the "Ocean of Love-Intelligence," and there is nothing personal about them. They belong to the Mind of God, and there is one essential existentially valid idea out of which the others find their source: it is the idea (the truth "formula") of Oneness — God and man the spiritual being are already one, and there is no life or mind apart from the Divine Life, the One Mind. "God and His creation are one" (Thomas Hora). Once we can identify the difference between the two pools of ideations, we can choose to entertain thoughts from this existentially valid pool. The presence of God-confirmatory thoughts in our consciousness has the beneficial effect of gradually obliterating the self-confirmatory thoughts. Since God is the eternal Being of our being, the eternal Life of our life, the eternal Mind of our mind, it is not possible to "not be." As we come to see our inseparability from God, our fears and anxieties can be healed. God-confirmatory thoughts support and keep us increasingly assured in the truth-of-being; they invite us to be inspired, creative and insightful, enhance our abilities and talents, and translate into healing and goodness in our human experience. Consciousness is blessed and enlightened by these divine ideas, which glorify God, but we are not responsible for producing them. The term, *ideation*, depersonalizes the intelligent, the beautiful and true, giving all the credit to God, the only Source of all Intelligence, Love and Good. The Zen directive "Erase yourself utterly" takes on new meaning. In a God-confirmatory consciousness, as Dr. Hora so eloquently stated it, "There is no self or other — there is only the awareness of God's perfect Reality revealing Itself in all life forms in absolute perfection and beauty." Man can be aware of God as a self-revealing Presence of Love and Intelligence in his life and be grateful and joyous. As our interest becomes focused on "what really is" — God really Is — our childhood conditioning to see ourselves as persons (defined by our parents' thoughts about us) can be gradually dissolved. We will be able to know our authentic identity, and to see the only "I AM" and ourselves as Its individualized manifestations. Dwelling in the righteous thoughts of God-confirmatory ideation is all we will ever need to maintain us in Perfect Life — now and forever. "How precious are thy thoughts unto me, O God!" (Ps. 139:17).

> Only God's thoughts constitute my true being.
> — Thomas Hora

Interaction

Interaction is thinking about what other people are thinking about what we are thinking; it is a horizontal and psychological perspective on life which is preoccupied with relationship thinking and invites interpersonal friction. Interaction fills us with incessant mental chatter: it is wondering how we are "doing," if we said the "right" thing, speculating if we are liked or disliked. Interaction thoughts keep our perspective on "self and other," locked in the dream state of interpersonal life, leaving us struggling with relationships.

The source of all our human suffering and problems is interaction thoughts and self-confirmatory ideation. They go together and emanate from the "sea of mental garbage;" therefore, we must learn to refuse to let these thoughts take root in our consciousness. Since interaction is based on the false impression that there are many minds and many powers in the world, it encourages the belief in an existence apart from the divine Source, and it tempts us to live and act from that misperception. Living from this false perception of ourselves hypnotizes us into one mistaken idea after another. Since interaction thinking is always

> All problems are psychological...
>
> –- *Thomas Hora*

interpersonal, it can also take the form of reaction or nonaction; it is the mental static which interferes with our ability to see oneness and remain in Omniaction. This kind of thinking manifests in us as "shoulds," as anxiety and worry, fear, ruminations, fantasies, romantic dreams; as bragging, talking too much, looking for approval and attention; as influencing, manipulation, bribery, trespassing, gossip; as blame, guilt, criticism, anger, confrontations, arguments; as assumptions, speculations, confusion, expectations, disappointments, grievances and trouble, and as all forms of sexual activity. Interaction is always seeking experiences with other persons — in thought or activity. Interaction causes us to make judgments, express opinions, compare ourselves to others, explain and justify ourselves and to be mentally preoccupied with what kind of impression we are making, how we are perceived in our jobs, families and communities. It can drive us and others "crazy." It can also manifest in less dramatic but irritating ways, as asking a lot of personal questions, being nosy, inquisitive, curious or a busybody, as ingratiating behavior or "helping" when unbidden. Even interaction thinking which could be considered pleasant can leave us ultimately unfulfilled, because interaction (which is person-oriented) distracts us from God's omniactive Presence and the peace and assurance which we can know when we are not engaged in interaction. A by-product of interaction thinking is fatigue and even exhaustion. It is important to know that interaction thinking can also manifest as a *symptom* (which Metapsychiatry defines as *an interaction thought*) or *pain* (which Metapsychiatry defines as *an angry interaction thought*). We are clarifying that these pains or symptoms are just thoughts we are experiencing organismically. Certain kinds of habitually entertained interaction thoughts tend to channel themselves into the body, and then appear as sickness, illness and even disease. Metapsychiatry has identified that interpersonal thinking can ultimately manifest pathogenically. However, once the specific nature of an interaction thought is discerned and replaced by some aspect of spiritual knowledge, the symptom can disappear. We are grateful to know that our body (and the body of our experience) can be healed by understanding the harmful dynamic of interaction thinking.

Interaction thinking gives us the harmful impression that what goes on between people is what constitutes real life, but it is not. It is only the "dream of life in personhood," which preoccupies us with infinitely different ways to confirm our apparent self-existence. We will never be free of interaction as long as we believe ourselves to be autonomous persons interacting with other autonomous persons. We will never be free of interaction as long as we are participating in an illusion of separate minds and separate mind power, which distract us from seeing Omniaction. We all tend to take interpersonal life too seriously — it wastes our precious energy and vitiates our purpose here. But we can eventually come to see that in this worldly, dimensional life, it only "seems to be" that there is interaction; the illusion of this worldly life is convincing in that it is visible. Actually, in divine Reality there is "no self or other" to interact — there is only the action of the One Mind and One Power, which is infinitely good, supremely loving and always intelligent, expressing Itself as Omniaction, unconditionally and nonpersonally, through Its individualizations. Omniaction means God is the only activating power of all that is real and good in the whole universe. Contemplating Principle #3 of Metapsychiatry can help to lift us out of the darkness of interaction thinking. Being more interested in beholding Omniaction requires us to see there is only the good of God going on right now, here and everywhere, and then we can begin to abolish the unreality of the phenomenal world and its dream experiences

> ...all solutions are spiritual.
> —- *Thomas Hora*

in our consciousness. If we are still suffering from an old interaction experience, all that is happening is that we are unable to disengage from the thought we are entertaining about it. So what we failed to respond to yesterday or ten years ago, we can respond to now — correcting the invalid thought around that experience (thereby disengaging from it) and replacing it with a valid thought of spiritual understanding — and the whole situation can be healed. Interaction thinking is time-bound, but its healing spiritual counterfact (Omniaction) is timeless — this means, Its activity is not constrained by the laws of this world. It can dissolve any event which has occurred in human consciousness and has manifested in this illusory world since the beginning of time. "The understanding of what really is abolishes all that seems to be" (Principle #10 of Metapsychiatry). Ultimately, we all have to forgive ourselves and others for what really never happened in the dream of life in interaction. When we have finally obliterated the illusion in our own consciousness, that there is a finite world inhabited by physical persons, we will no longer be available to interaction thoughts and all the disturbances they manifest.

Omniaction

OMNIACTION is the harmonizing movement of Spirit through human affairs (from Latin, *omnes* = all, everywhere + active). The omnipresent, omniscient, omnipotent activity of divine Love-Intelligence is in all ways everywhere active, and this invisible mental Force is everywhere expressing Itself through all individuals, governing our lives through inspired wisdom and love, adjusting, correcting, harmonizing and healing.

The whole universe is under divine control and power. But we do not normally see it until we are awakened. All Wisdom and Truth and Love and Energy come from the Divine Mind. It is only through cultivating spiritual awareness that we can come to see "what really is," not what should be or what should not be. Awakened man sees life in the context of Omniaction where there is no self or other: there is only God as this vital self-revealing Force, actively pressing for manifestation in every life form — in every leaf, every blade of grass, every flower, and in every consciousness. Spirit is an irrepressible Force which lives Life through us. This means that, in truth, the business of life is not really between persons — not interconnected, interpersonal or interrelated — but between each of us and God. When we are letting God's ideas, clarity, truth and love "obtain" and speak through us — verbally or nonverbally — we are engaged in existentially valid communication and not in interaction. Even though it seems as if man is communicating to man, it is not so because man does not produce thoughts — he only receives them. Man's consciousness is dwelling in either the self-confirmatory, phenomenal world or the God-confirmatory, divine Reality. Thus, only God is communicating to man and through man as existentially valid ideas — anything else is interpersonal dreaming from the "sea of mental garbage." So, in truth, all that is real is a "joint participation in the good of God." Realizing the presence of Omniaction encourages us to see oneness, a life wholly dependent on the divine Source. The existence of this dynamic Principle, as an activity of the One Mind, invites us to go beyond phenomena and the material world to see God flowing freely through us and through others as Its individualized ("undivided") manifestations.

> There is no existence apart from God,
> and there is no God apart from His creation.
>
> — Thomas Hora

Omniaction is always operating and always in control — regardless of any appearances to the contrary. Omniaction is an immutable, indestructible Principle, a Law, which we can lean on with complete assurance, just as we do the law of gravity. Understanding Its dynamism invites It to heal any unpleasant or disturbing interaction experience we have ever had in the dream of life in interaction — astonishingly, all the interactions since the beginning of time could be abolished in the moment that an individual really understands the power of the Principle of Omniaction and the Perfect Harmony It bestows. "Every valley shall be lifted up, and every mountain and hill be made low, the uneven ground shall become level, and the rough places a plain. And the glory of the Lord shall be revealed..." (Is. 40:44-5) as Omniaction moves throughout the Earth.

Erase your self utterly

Erase your self utterly

Erase your self utterly

Erase your self utterly

Erase your self utterly

Erase your self utterly

Erase your self utterly

Erase your self utterly

Erase your self utt

Erase your self

Erase your

Erase

Erase

Erase

OPERATIONALISM is a self-confirmatory and interactive approach to life which involves calculative and horizontal thinking and cause-and-effect thinking, and which is concerned with how to do things; the operational perspective is concerned with the activity of "doing" — with personal effort, personal willfulness, ambitiousness, mastery and control, with influencing, persuading, convincing, networking, planning, coping, "handling" situations, "fixing" things, changing peoples' behavior, manipulating (being an "operator") and bribing — and which is ignorant of the all-governing Power and Presence of divine Love-Intelligence.

Dr. Hora summed up operationalism as "I can do it." Since operationalism excludes a knowledge of the real nature of God, of the Fundamental Order of Existence, and of ourselves as Its inseparable spiritual manifestations, it assumes that we have to do everything ourselves if we want to get it done. This approach operates out of the false belief that man is a self-existent personality with personal power and personal attributes and that he can act autonomously in the world. For instance, love cannot be done; intelligence cannot be done; inspiration and creativity cannot be done. We cannot produce love or intelligence, inspiration or creativity — we can only express them as divine attributes. Operationalism demonstrates a habit of "should" thinking, and it leads to

> Harmonious Action
> maintains control;
> exertion upsets the balance.
>
> — *Lao-tze*

fearfulness when its goals cannot be realized; it can leave us feeling tired or exhausted from the personal effort or exertion it requires as we try to make things work out a certain way. Jesus elucidated the difference between these terms, operationalism and existentialism, in the biblical story of Mary and Martha (Lk. 10:40-42). Martha, who "was distracted with much serving" and "should" thinking, was too busy to pay attention to Christ's message; Martha's approach to work and to life was self-confirmatory in nature, concerned with its own agenda, and unavailable to the spontaneity of the moment. Her prototype illustrates the operational mode of being-in-the-world. Mary, on the other hand, who was more interested in existential truth and spiritual blessedness than in "doing" and getting things accomplished, was free to pay attention to the Christ wisdom. Mary's approach to work and to life was God-confirmatory in nature. As we juxtapose these two modes of being, we can see Mary's as the existentially valid one. When we are listening to the Christ wisdom, we are able to respond to life's demands from a qualitatively different state of consciousness, one whereby "doing flows out of Being" (Lao-tze).

EXISTENTIALISM is a God-confirmatory and omniactive approach to life which cannot be "done"; the existential perspective is concerned with Being, with allowing divine inspiration and love to flow from God into consciousness in order to guide and govern its life. Existentialism is a term which encompasses the philosophical inquiry into the true nature of existence and the divine context in which it manifests itself. "God is love; and he that dwelleth in love dwelleth in God, and God in him" (I Jn. 4:16) and Dr. Hora's words, "God and His creation are one," crystallize the essence of Existential Metapsychiatry.

The etymology of existence (from Latin, *ex-*, out + *sistere,* to cause to stand) reveals that man possesses a faculty of consciousness (the *transcendent observer*) which enables him to be aware of standing out or apart. This faculty allows him to be a nonpersonal observer of his own experiences and thought processes and thereby to transcend himself. Man must be able to see himself from a transcendent perspective in order to understand himself correctly — to know the "I AM THAT I AM" (Ex. 3:14). Existentialism seeks to understand what man is as a divine being, what the meaning and purpose of his existence is, what the spiritual laws which govern his existence are, and what knowledge is needed so that he can learn to live in harmony with spiritual laws and be in alignment with the Fundamental Order of Existence. Existentialism asks: "What is

> Man reveals the existence of Existence. Without a background, the foreground could not stand out.
>
> — Thomas Hora

real, and what is not real?" "What is truth, health, good, evil, disease, death?" Existential Metapsychiatry is interested in uncovering the one eternal Life, the invisible background — "what really is" — which we call Spiritual Reality and which reveals Itself in contrast to the visible foreground — "what seems to be." Again, we can see how useful "what is not" can be to allow us to see "what is." Before we can discover what is right and what works, we may first have to find out what is not right and what does not work. As Dr. Hora taught us, "Life is a school where there is a single subject: Reality."

The existential viewpoint awakens us to realize the truth-of-being as spiritual even while we are moving through a material, finite world, offering us the opportunity for transformation, healing, redemption and liberation, here and now — and not in some future Kingdom. The existential approach manifests as a quality of life that is radically different from the operational one. It requires that we abide by Principle #5 of Metapsychiatry, "God helps those who let Him" (i.e., those who let God be God under all circumstances). In this way, our living becomes effortless, efficient and effective (the "three Es"). Jesus, who could be called the greatest existentialist, urged us to take his "yoke" — the Christ teaching and spiritual perspective — upon us, making our existence "easy" and "light" (Mt. 11:29-30). As Rumi says, "Mystics are experts in laziness. They rely on it because they consistently see God working all around them. The harvest keeps coming in, yet they never even did the plowing" (Rumi).

EXPERIENCE is a conscious or unconscious thought which is organismically perceived. Thoughts entertained in consciousness manifest themselves in words or actions, and these words or actions, in turn, have a tendency to attract corresponding experiences (Principle #7 of Metapsychiatry, aka, The Law of Correspondence or The Law of Attraction).

Metapsychiatry identifies three kinds of experiences, and they all occur in the organism: the Intellectual, which takes place in the brain; the emotional, which takes place in the neurovegetative system; the sensory, which takes place in the sense organs. Experiencing, therefore, means intellectual, emotional and sensual stimulation, and persons see these as synonymous with "life," with "living." Unawakened, we tend to think the good of life inheres in experiencing; the love of feeling good and having pleasurable experiences is universally accepted as a valid pursuit. An orientation towards experiencing reveals that we see ourselves solely as biological organisms and not as spiritual beings. God knows nothing of our experiences — experiences belong to the dream state of the human condition, and do not constitute Reality. "At night, we dream in pictures, and, during the day, we dream in experiences" (Thomas Hora). Even evil is only an experience, a frightful or dreadful one, but an experience

> At night, we dream in pictures, and during the day, we dream in experiences.
>
> — *Thomas Hora*

nonetheless. Real life is not dreaming; real life is not experiencing. Real life is nondimensional existence, and it cannot be perceived experientially: it can only be realized in an awakened consciousness. As we wake up to the truth-of-being, we gradually lose interest in our experiences, both pleasurable and not pleasurable. This means that events will come to our attention, but no longer into our experience. We will be able to respond to experiences, even if they are disturbing, dispassionately and with compassion, without being upset, reactive or troubled. Experiences belong to the phenomenal world of duality, of opposites, so they can be good or bad, pleasurable or painful, involve gain or loss. This dynamic reveals experiences to be existentially invalid pursuits (which rob us of our life-energy and often leave us exhausted). Experiences always involve interaction and self-confirmatory preoccupations. Experiences are always transitory and are, therefore, impermanent — they do not endure. We may experience many experiences without ever learning or realizing anything. Even though "experiencing" and "realizing" are words which are often used interchangeably, they are not the same. Experiencing is of the flesh and occurs in the realm of the material world — realization is of the spirit and occurs in the realm of consciousness.

REALIZATION is a cognitive event occurring spontaneously in consciousness when some aspect of transcendent Reality becomes real to us or is "seen"; it is a synonym for understanding, and it is inspired. A realization comes to us by grace of God, and is transformative and healing to our perspective on life. "It is the spirit in a man, the breath of the Almighty, that makes him understand" (Job. 32:8).

Once we realize some aspect of Truth, it is ours forever — it endures. For instance, every time we really understand the answer to the second intelligent question, we are blessed. Realizing is not organismic — it does not occur in the brain or body — it occurs as a higher form of awareness in consciousness. When inspired wisdom touches our consciousness, the temporal-spatial coordinates of experience are suspended — we are in timelessness which can have a very beneficial effect. And, with every realization of some aspect of spiritual knowledge, our consciousness is gradually ascending. We are actually beginning to see and understand spiritual principles and discovering truth for ourselves. A realization is an epiphany, a spiritual awakening to what already exists but has been hitherto unseen by us (Principle #9 of Metapsychiatry). An epiphany is a moment of divine revelation when a "light" from above breaks into human experience, when something previously unknown or misperceived is able to be clearly seen by us. Truth, divine Love-Intelligence, is no longer an abstract; and, once it has been apprehended, it can be transmuted into whatever form is needed to help us in our experience.

> Be ye not conformed to this world,
> but be ye transformed
> by the renewal of your mind.
>
> — Ro. 12:2

While experiences occur in the temporal and corporeal realm, realizations of divine Reality and seeing ourselves as Its manifestations, occur in the transcendent realm of consciousness, outside of time and beyond flesh. Experiences and realizations are not synonymous (but realizations can manifest as a transformation in our experiential life). It is helpful to know that, mostly, experiences are eventually disintegrative in quality, especially those which involve pleasure and excitement. Realizations, on the other hand, are essentially integrative in quality, establishing the contents of our consciousness in divine existence and in existentially valid values, which are always life-affirming and health-promoting. Until the difference between them is understood, it will be difficult to grasp the truth of ourselves as spiritual beings, and God will remain a distant concept. Using the process of juxtaposition helps us to see more — using what is worldly to reveal what is divine. Jesus said: "That which is born of the flesh is flesh; that which is born of the Spirit is spirit[ual]" (Jn. 3:6). Being "born of the Spirit" is the revelation that our true substance is spiritual, not physical, that we are creations of God, not of our parents, conceived in the divine Mind and brought forth from the "womb" of Consciousness.

Person

PERSON is the self-existent, self-motivated, self-energized, self-propelled, independent entity which we all pretend to be.

The etymology of person is enlightening (from the Latin, *per*, by + *sona*, sound). This derivation is attributed to the Greek tragedies where the actors' faces were covered by masks, corresponding to the emotion or emotions being portrayed, which meant that the actors could only be truly identified by the sounds of their voices. This word derivation points to the idea that our true identities are masked by our appearances and pretenses and our play-acting and that our true vibrations can be discerned beyond our visible form. Each "person" is a unique vibration of the I AM Presence. If our vibratory frequencies (the contents of our consciousness) are "in tune" with the Divine, we are manifesting harmony; if our vibratory frequencies (the contents of our consciousness) are not "in tune" with the Divine, the disharmony can be perceived, regardless of our masks. But, in either case, the tangibility of our physicality tends to hide the intangibility of our true identities as spiritual — our unique, divine vibration — which has led us to imagine that we exist apart from God. It "seems to be" that we are material persons, but we are really spiritual beings, masquerading as phenomena. God never created "persons;" God knows nothing of "persons," (or matter or dimensionality) and, as the Bible says, "God is

> Let God be true,
> though every man [is] a liar...
> — Ro. 3:4

no respecter of persons" (Acts 10:34). God created each of us "in his own image...and after his own likeness" (Gn. 1:26,27), as nondimensional consciousness whose substance, like God's, is spirit. We must remember, we are defined by God, not the other way around. Coming to understand this truth does not negate the physical "experience" of individual existence in the phenomenal world; it only abolishes the concepts of "persons" and "personhood" as real and important. As these "persons" we seem to be, we have personalities, personal reactions, personal opinions, personal experiences, personal histories and interpersonal relationships — and we personalize everything, whether it is ignorance or truth. The basis of personhood involves being very preoccupied with making something of ourselves, so we can be better persons and more important persons than other persons. But all this is a dream which distracts us from discovering the truth-of-being. Seeing ourselves only as psychological or physical persons is a misperception of Reality; we are "judging by appearances" and experiences and living from our senses, which leads us to false conclusions. Our appearance implies separateness and gives rise to the mistaken impression that we are self-created persons with minds and wills of our own, with talents and gifts of our own, attributes and faculties of our own, acting independently from any Deity. The belief in an existence apart from God is demonstrated in the collective illusion of personhood. But the Bible corrects this idea, informing us, we are "without father, or mother or genealogy, and [have] neither beginning of days nor end of life..." (Heb. 7:3). Contemplating the Zen koan, "Show me the face which you had before your parents were born," can help to expand our consciousness beyond life in a finite dimensional context, so that we can really come to know the meaning of the eternal words, "Never born, never dying" (Heb. 7:3). It is necessary to become interested in seeing more than meets the eye, to begin to awaken to the understanding of the mystics which sees that this material world is a dream we are collectively dreaming, to see that it is hiding an invisible, perfect Realm and our perfect, "birthless and deathless," invisible life in It. We discover our true being in the context of God when we can see our hidden identity as eternal and spiritual substance, when we can understand our place and purpose in the universe, not as a person, but as an individualized presence through which the Presence of God can reveal Itself in infinite

META Meanings

Page 44

ways. Dr. Hora beautifully elevates our vision with these words: "God created a perfect universe and 'peopled' it with perfect, spiritual reflections of Himself."

 # Presence

PRESENCE is the quality of consciousness present; it is a "place" where Divine Love-Intelligence can reveal Itself; it is an individualization of the divine Presence; it is the "I am" presence of the "I AM" Presence (Ex. 3:14); **it is a nondimensional transparency through which the good of God can shine into the world.**

As we awaken to become conscious of our spiritual identities, able to discern spiritual values and truth and to appreciate them, the limited concept of person is gradually replaced by the limitless concept of a nonpersonal eternal presence. Presence points beyond visible form to the invisible, spiritualized contents of consciousness —

> We must refuse to be human and insist on being spiritual.
>
> — *Thomas Hora*

it is able to reveal itself to us in juxtaposition to personality. This means we become increasingly aware of the existence of presence within us as we identify the personality we believe ourselves to be and the truth-of-being begins to dissolve it and transform us. Person belongs to the finite, material, dream-world of phenomena — presence reflects the infinite, nonmaterial, divine Reality. They are qualitatively different. The quality of a presence is discernible through the "vibrations" (or "vibes") it emanates, and ultimately by what the consciousness values — what it cherishes, hates and fears. Every individual presence has the inherent ability to reveal God's Infinite Presence in the world as an individualized aspect of It, once the consciousness has been purified of its mistaken identity and spiritualized through right knowledge. (The word *individual*, derived from Latin, *individua*, means *undivided*, and the word *identity*, derived from Latin, *idem*, means the *same or like*.) The more we can come to see our identities as the same as God and our undividedness in all its divine aspects, the more we are living consciously as spiritual beings. The more an individual is interested to know what it means to be "here for God," the more he will be able to shed personality traits and human characteristics and, thus, realize his essential and authentic identity as presence. Like the rays of the sun which show forth the qualities of the sun — warmth, radiance and power — so can each of us as a transparency emanate all the spiritual qualities of God — goodness, love, intelligence, peace, vitality, assurance, joy, harmony, freedom, wisdom, compassion. The infinite potential of the Infinite Presence is always available to each of us as an infinite presence — this means, even "greater works than these [than the Christ demonstrated] shall you do" (Jn. 14:12). As a consciousness is gradually cleansed through prayer and practice, the false sense of the person diminishes and the beauty of the presence can emerge. "He [the Christ presence] must increase, but I [personal identity] must decrease" (Jn. 3:30).

MODES OF BEING-IN-THE-WORLD is a Metapsychiatric term (originating with the philosopher, Heidegger) to describe a quality of existence which is actually determined by an individual's main mental preoccupations: by the prevailing thought patterns, cherished values and belief systems which constitute the contents of one's consciousness.

This term is central to Meta-work because Metapsychiatry does not treat persons — it treats modes of being-in-the-world. Whatever a human being values is what will determine his mode of being-in-the-world. "As a man thinketh in his heart, so is he" (Pr. 23:7). The "heart" points to what we cherish. Mostly, unenlightened man cherishes pleasure, but he can also value money, possessions, children, job identity, personal recognition and influence, power, status, cleverness, intellectual superiority, his so-called talents and skills, good looks, sex, experiences, excitement, sports, travel, food, clothes, to identify a few. The emphasis here is not on persons or psychological labels, but on consciousness and its contents, on how these externalize as the way we function in the world and are perceived, and as the concrete "reality" which we experience. ("Modes of being" are not to be confused with life-styles, which are operational and concern behavior.) Therefore, a mode of being-in-the-world is identified by discerning its main mental themes, i.e., the habitual thought patterns it entertains and in which it dwells, and how these manifest as that individual's experience. Our mode-of-being is reflected back to us by our experiences in the world, and this dynamic helps us to see "our" thoughts, allowing us to cleanse them. "As within, so without." Metapsychiatry identifies three main modes of being-in-the-world:

1. being here for oneself;
2. being here for others;
3. being here for God.

The first two modes-of-being are existentially invalid and demonstrate in an infinite variety of troublesome forms which leave God out of the picture. The last, and only existentially valid, mode-of-being is "being here for God." It is essentially an ego-less mode, flowing out of an enlightened consciousness, the result of its gradual spiritualization as its contents have been corrected and healed, i.e., replaced by spiritual understanding. Metapsychiatry consistently encourages us to direct and redirect our attention and orientation to "being here for God" because it is what lifts consciousness out of self-confirmatory and interactive preoccupations, and eventually erases our invalid modes of being-in-the-world. "I have made you for myself that you may show forth my glory" (Is. 43:21). So, as we come to cherish and appreciate existentially valid values as synonymous with divine attributes — such as love, intelligence, vitality, assurance, peace, joy, gratitude, receptivity and responsiveness, harmony, order, creativity, inspiration and freedom — we are filled with their presence. It is the Presence of these values in our consciousness which transforms our modes of being-in-the-world. Ultimately, "being here for God" translates into a "beneficial presence" in the world because it is the *built-in intentionality* of each of us to reveal God in every simple moment of our lives.

BENEFICIAL PRESENCE is one who is "here for God," the eventual and only existentially valid mode of being-in-the-world; it is a highly enlightened consciousness which is in the world as a model of spiritual excellence and compassion, the equivalent of a bodhisattva.

A beneficial presence is influential by the quality of his or her consciousness; he or she does not "do" anything; he or she is an open channel, a clear individualization of the I AM Presence, embodying and living the right values. This individual is not attached to people nor detached from them; he or she is neither personal nor aloof; this presence neither condemns nor condones and does not engage in personal reactions; this divine consciousness is responsive to manifest needs in an intelligent and compassionate way. A beneficial presence is filled to the brim with divine Love and Intelligence, with PAGL, and it glows from his or her being. Jesus "glowed" to such an extent that his whole body was filled with light. This state of consciousness has been gradually washed clean of all polluting, self-confirmatory values and false beliefs and has cultivated a deep appreciation for spiritual truth. This individual has gained a point of immunity in consciousness whereby he or she can identify and refuse the world's hypnotic suggestions and lie-messages about the nature of reality. This spiritual being knows that our love, intelligence and vitality have a

> A beneficial presence glows for God.
>
> — *Thomas Hora*

transcendent derivation; and it shines these divine lights of love, intelligence, joy and fearlessness into the world, confirming the presence of God. In the Zen tradition, it is said that "wherever an enlightened consciousness goes, even the dead trees come alive." Thus, a beneficial presence is a blessing wherever it goes by virtue of the spiritually illumined quality of its consciousness. Everyone needs to be seen as a "living soul," and a beneficial presence can impart this gift to all on whom his or her thoughts rest or with whom he or she makes contact. This individual is a focal point of harmony and healing, a transparency through which the "good of God" can be seen and expressed. This dynamic can occur because an individual has realized incorporeal life and the biblical definition of itself as an "image" and "likeness" (Gn. 1:27) of God. This individual can, therefore, achieve the optimal fulfillment of his divine potential. A beneficial presence is an authentic expression of the attributes of God and reflects the emerging Christ-consciousness or Buddha-nature. "Let this mind be in you, which was also in Christ Jesus" (Ph. 2:5).

PHENOMENAL WORLD is interaction and self-confirmatory thoughts appearing in visible form as the material universe; it is the realm of "form and formlessness," of fantasies and dreams, of relationship thinking, of "what seems to be." This sphere is the realm of dualistic thinking; it is the world of opposites and, as such, is a corruption of nondual Good; it is dimensional, of the senses, and the illusion of personal mind and personal mind power; it is the world of symbolic structures — everything in the material world is a symbolic statement — either about God, which is Truth and Reality, or about unreality, illusion and falsehood.

Dr. Hora defined the world with these words: "The world appears to be something massive and serious, tangible, material and impressive, but it is only thoughts — the universe emerges from thoughts." It is the outpicturing of "our" thoughts — a dream which we are collectively dreaming. And our individual "world" is the manifestation of whatever we cherish, whatever we hate (or love to hate), whatever we fear (or love to fear). Dr. Hora goes on to say, "But this impressive, tangible world of appearances is not Reality — it is the shadow of Reality, pointing beyond itself to true substance which is spiritual." A shadow is an imperfect representation of what is real, a counterfeit of it; it is an imitation or a copy, a dark reflection, an optical illusion. This world, call it "shadow" or "counterfeit," is not authentic and not substantial; it just "seems to be." It is illusory and designed to deceive us into believing it is real and substantial and that we are self-existing persons, separate and apart from God, with minds and wills and lives of our own. This world needs to be understood as a mirror of divine Reality: it reflects the real, but it is not real. The phenomenal world is the experience of the illusory idea of separation. Phenomena are just garbage thoughts appearing as form and formlessness. The problem is, Hora warns us: "We confuse God's Perfect, Invisible Creation with the forms through which It emanates, and it gives us the impression that God has created the form life."

When Adam and Eve, desiring to be "like God" (Gn. 3) and to become "wise," were seduced by the serpentine thought to satisfy their wants outside of God, the illusory world of "good and evil" appeared. This appearance is the manifestation of a false belief that we could become "like God" and live independently. We are "God-like," in His [Its] "image" and "likeness," but we are not independently powerful like God. If we understand that God is the only power, and there is no separation between God and Its emanations, we will begin to see this world as the counterfeit it is, a place where we all struggle to make it on our own. The problem is that this world of appearances is fabricated on a lie, and this lie — the thought of separation — took form as the physical bodies of our prototypes, Adam and Eve. Because "thoughts manifest as our experience," the world of the separate-self appeared when we believed ourselves to have a mind and a life of our own — and we are still living this misperception daily. This misperception is the source of all self-confirmatory ideation and interaction thinking, holding us hostage in a dream. Because the illusion has distorted the truth-of-being and is always working to support the belief in separation, man dreams that he has power to think, to do, to control — to be "like God." And because he is not God, he is actually an imposter, as Dr. Hora said, "a miscreator." He distorts the ideas which flow to him from God's "Garden of Eden Consciousness[1]," and uses them to glorify and gratify himself, to exert so-called personal power and influence in the world, to serve greed and materialism, to confirm himself and others through interpersonal relationship thinking, because the foundation idea of this world is based on the serpentine lie of an autonomous self. (Metapsychiatry calls this belief in self-existence the "Adamic perspective.") Because man is not God, he has no power to "create" either good or evil or a perfect life. Only God, the One Mind, creates, and what It creates is always good without an opposite. So man, the "miscreator," receiving thoughts from the "sea of mental garbage" suffers the consequences, and his world demonstrates "flipsides": the "good" here is material, a counterfeit good, and has a built-in opposite — every pleasure can invite pain; every gain can invite loss. This tangible world reflects "darkly" and imperfectly its divine counterpart:

> Spiritual Reality is perfect nondual Good — the phenomenal world is imperfect and dualistic in nature.
> Spiritual Reality is made up of nondimensional, nonmaterial and noumenal substance — the world is
> made up of dreams manifesting as dimensionality, matter and phenomena.
> The "Ocean of Love-Intelligence" is the dwelling place of God — the "sea of mental garbage" is
> the dwelling place of ignorance.
> Spiritual Reality is infinite and eternal Life — the phenomenal world is
> the finite and transitory experience of birth and death.

Now, perhaps, it is possible to examine the idea that this shadow world is made up of "symbolic structures": symbolic structures are counterfeits of Spiritual Reality, or distortions of It, appearing in the phenomenal world as matter. When we believe the symbols — the appearances and experiences of this world, including the myths, legends, historical data, facts and information — to be real and important, instead of discerning what they "point" to, we are distracted by them, misinformed, and arrive at false conclusions about the real nature of existence. All phenomena falsify the truth-of-being. Our form-identity (i.e., our body), for example, is a symbolic structure, a misleading image about who and what we are. Not perceiving the divine ideas to which forms point, we confuse these "symbolic structures" with Reality, thinking they are real unto themselves — for instance, thinking that physicality is what is real about us. Zen tradition warns us, "The finger pointing to the moon is not the moon." So we must see beyond the structure to its real substance. For example, a flower is not beauty — a flower points to the infinite presence of Beauty — a flower is beautiful only because God's beauty is everywhere present; music, which is intangible but palpable, points to the laws of Harmony and Order and reflects the rhythm of the universe; time is a symbolic structure pointing to the perfect order and "timeliness" of God's universe; even a lamp can be seen as a symbolic structure pointing to real Light and its ability to dissolve darkness when it is "plugged in," i.e., aware of its source; an acorn points us to become aware of the hidden truth that the entire fulfillment of our creative potential and divine purpose exists already within each of us; and, our faculties, such as our eyes and ears and mind, are not "our" autonomous faculties, but individualized symbolic aspects of the One All-Seeing, All-Knowing Mind. We call symbolic structures the "shadows" of Reality, inviting us to see what specific aspect of the invisible and perfect divine Life they are intimating. Everything on this Earth that is healthy, beautiful, good, helping us and uplifting the spirit, is a divine inspiration, idea or faculty in visible form (a symbolic structure) pointing to the existence of God. However, by virtue of the fact that everything in this world of opposites is subject to the human "laws of sin and death" (Ro. 8:2), everything in form is therefore finite and corruptible. Since the divine ideas of God, entertained by man, the "miscreator," are distorted by him to serve his own self-glorifying, materialistic ends, they result in wars, poverty, disease and natural disasters. They are the destructive contents of the "sea of mental garbage," manifestations of the ignorance and arrogance of the collective consciousness, amassing and taking form as the dualistic experiences of an illusory world.

To behold and realize Reality beyond these images requires us to turn away from the shadows, to see through them, in order to transcend the collective dream of the world of appearances. Jesus advised us to "Be passers by" (Thomas, logia 42) and also revealed to us that the Kingdom of the Christ is "not of this world" (Jn. 18:36). The enlightened Christ-consciousness is not involved in or distracted by the value system of this world. It dwells in an invisible, timeless, perfect realm where a different system of values applies. It has come to realize that it has never left the "Garden of Eden Consciousness." The Christ, the Buddha, Lao-tze and the great wisdom teachers understood the mystical nature of the universe and had awakened to see that this material realm was not the real one. When Jesus spoke of "overcoming the world" (Jn. 16:33), he was pointing to the possibility which exists within consciousness to go beyond the limits of life in matter and in the fleshly existence in order to find a Higher Reality which lies beyond this one. But we need to know the nature of this world before we can be freed of its spell and interested in transcending it. Neither flesh nor the senses have access to this spiritual Universe, this "Kingdom" of which Christ spoke, but consciousness, made of Its same substance, has access to It at every holy instant. We can see once again that the worldly experience is useful — leaning on it and experiencing all its imperfections forces us to look beyond it to the nonmaterial Reality. We will then no longer be defined by the world, even though everything in this world is always trying to define us, limit us, and imprison us in its mockery of oneness. In the end, everything except God is a metaphor.

Holographic research postulates that the whole world is really transparent and all material structures are not what they seem to be — they are actually insubstantial, like shadows. Quantum theory points to the discovery of a supremely intelligent order which is operating beyond our vision, but which is underlying and pervading this world. This means that quantum physics sees a "universe," sometimes referred to as a "Field" of perfect Life, beyond the material one we know so well. It governs all life — everything is in It and It is in everything. This invisible "Field" of Intelligence and Presence, of Power, Order and Harmony, transcends the known physical universe. So, if we could see with a "quantum eye," we would see that we are already living in the Kingdom of God — and It is living in us, through us and as us, just as It lives in and through every flower, every blade of grass and every singing bird. We are simply unconscious of Its immanence and Its ever-present dynamism. We are "living in forgetfulness of Being" (Eckhart Tolle), asleep in the world of appearances, "seeing through a mirror dimly" (I Cor. 13:12). As Jesus told us, "...The Kingdom of the Father is spread throughout the earth, and no one sees it" (Thomas, logia 113). The substance of this Kingdom is perfect spiritual laws and principles, supporting, infusing and animating the all-in-All, which thankfully includes this shadow world. "This is not the real Reality. The real Reality is behind the curtain. In truth, we are not here — this is our shadow" (Rumi).

> **The world is every high thing that exalteth itself against the knowledge of God.**
> — II Cor. 10:5

SPIRITUAL REALITY is the infinite Presence of God; It is Cosmic Consciousness whose substance is Spirit; It is omniactive Divine Mind; God and Its Kingdom; Truth; Love-Intelligence; Being; Existence; Heaven; Paradise; the "Promised Land"; the Land of PAGL; indestructible unstoppable Life; the Eternal One and the only real dwelling place of every individual consciousness forever; It is "what really is," the nondimensional, nonmaterial, invisible existence beyond "form and formlessness," beyond space and time, the eternal Now. Eckhart Tolle calls it the "Infinite Field of Awareness," and quantum physics calls it "Nonlocal Mind." It is present everywhere but visible nowhere (now-here).

This perfect Realm is not to be confused with the phenomenal world of experiential life and sense-existence which is neither real nor perfect. However, It does pervade this imperfect world and maintain it, breaking through every life form that lets It. The substance of this Realm is nondual Goodness, constituted of spiritual values, spiritual qualities and divine laws which are always operating — in short, all the nondimensional attributes of God which maintain and sustain us and are made visible through us. The ideas and activities of perfect Love and supreme Intelligence are the essence of this Domain, and spiritual blessedness is the divine fruit we receive when we partake of It. Nondimensional, noumenal Reality cannot be apprehended by the fleshly mind or the sensory organs. It is not tangible or visible, and It cannot be experienced or imagined, measured or quantified. It is inconceivable and unfathomable to the human mind; yet It is knowable to

> God did not create a perfect world —
> God created a perfect spiritual Universe.
> — *Thomas Hora*

spiritual man who, as an "image" and "likeness" of God and an emanation of this Reality, has the inherent capacity to discern It spiritually, once awakened to It. A spiritual being can recognize and identify It by the evidence of Its Presence, and can eventually behold It everywhere. "To the illumined mind, the whole world burns and sparkles with light" (Ralph Waldo Emerson). As a consciousness is gradually purified of the "garbage" thoughts of self-confirmatory and interaction thinking and is ascending out of the world's influences, it becomes increasingly spiritualized by the light of divine understanding and can come to realize aspects of this Kingdom of God in its own life. Dr. Hora's words, "Let us live in the humble expectancy of a perfect Universe gradually revealing Itself to us, until we know and see everything as it really is," encourage us to keep looking until we behold It. At this point, we have entered PAGL and can know bliss consciousness. We can know we are in contact with Reality (God) by the evidence of it in our lives, every time a healing, revelation, divine insight, inspiration, correction, adjustment, harmonizing solution or blessing descends into our lives. In this way, we are "tasting" (Ps. 34:8) the good of God and "seeing" Reality, not in some "afterlife," but in our everyday, ordinary experience.

Metapsychiatry's Prayer of Correct Self-Identification

God is not a person:	I am not a person.
God is Love:	I am friendly and nonpersonally, nonconditionally benevolent.
God is Mind:	I am intelligent.
God is Perfection:	I am healthy.
God is Life:	I am vitality.
God is Power:	I am strong and vigorous.
God is Infinite Mercy:	I am compassionate.
God is Goodness:	I am generous (in thought as well as in deed).
God is Joy:	I am joyful.
God is Peace:	I am peaceful.
God is the Divine Parent:	I am assured and safe forever.
God is Humor:	I am laughter and playfulness.
God is Constant and Never-Changing:	I am stable and trustworthy.
God is Infinity:	I am nondimensional spirit.
God is Eternity:	I am 'never born, never dying.'

God is the only "I AM" - I am because God is.
I and my Father are one.

The 11 Principles of Metapsychiatry

Principle #1
Thou shalt have no other interests before the good of God,
which is spiritual blessedness.

Principle #2
Take no thought for what should be or what should not be;
seek ye first to know the good of God, which already is.

Principle #3
There is no interaction anywhere;
there is only Omniaction everywhere.

Principle #4
Yes is good, but no is also good.

Principle #5
God helps those who let Him.

Principle #6
If you know what, you know how.

Principle #7
Nothing comes into experience uninvited.

Principle #8
Problems are lessons designed for our edification.

Principle #9
Reality cannot be experienced or imagined;
it can, however, be realized.

Principle #10
The understanding of "what really is"
abolishes all that "seems to be."

Principle #11
Do not show your pearls to unreceptive minds,
for they will demean them.

The meaning and purpose of life is to come
to know Reality.
— *Thomas Hora*

...This is life eternal [Reality]
that they might know thee
the only true God
and Jesus Christ
whom thou has sent.
— *Jn 17:3*

Everything material is finite,
and it dies.
But in Spiritual Reality,
there is no death.
— *Thomas Hora*

For as in Adam all die,
so in Christ shall all live.
— *I Cor. 15:22*

The way
that can be defined to death
is not the way to Life.
— *Tao Te Ching*

Published Works of Thomas Hora, M.D.

Books

Dialogues in Metapsychiatry
One Mind
Beyond the Dream
Existential Metapsychiatry
In Quest of Wholeness
Encounters with Wisdom

BOOKLETS

Can Meditation Be Done?
Commentaries on Scripture
Compassion
Forgiveness
God in Psychiatry
Healing through Spiritual Understanding
A Hierarchy of Values
Marriage and Family Life
Right Usefulness
Self-Transcendence
The Soundless Music of Life
What Does God Want?

Meditations from the Bible and the Works of Dr. Thomas Hora
Compiled by Joan Rubadeau, M.A.

For more information about Metapsychiatry and Thomas Hora's published works and audio library, visit **www.pagl.org.**

Metapsychiatry's books can be ordered from **www.amazon.com**

Published Works of Susan von Reichenbach

META Prayers and Principles
META Meanings
METAtations

METABooks can be ordered from **www.TheMetaWay.com**

Made in the USA
San Bernardino, CA
13 October 2018